Untold Jesus
The Two-Thousand-Year-Old Secret

by
Grant H. Pealer, D.D.

DORRANCE PUBLISHING CO., INC.
PITTSBURGH, PA 15222

All Rights Reserved
Copyright ©2002 by Grant H. Pealer, D.D.
No part of this book may be reproduced or transmitted
in any form or by any means, electronic or mechanical,
including photocopying, recording, or by any information
storage and retrieval system without permission in
writing from the publisher.

ISBN # 0-8059-5701-4
Printed in the United States of America

First Printing

For information or to order additional books, please write:
Dorrance Publishing Co., Inc.
643 Smithfield Street
Pittsburgh, Pennsylvania 15222
U.S.A.
1-800-788-7654
Or visit our web site and on-line catalog at *www.dorrancepublishing.com*

Dedication

In loving memory of my mother, Edna Worden Pealer (1925-1979), whose divine love, reaching across time and space, has proven that life never ends.

Introduction

Although the following text may seem strange to the reader, it should be understood this information is nothing new. Over the centuries, endless accounts have arisen which strongly suggest much of what we know of the Christian religion was based solely on the fables and outright lies produced by Saul of Tarsus. Add to this the endless tampering of the original story of Jesus by centuries of "adding to" or "taking from" Saul's account, and we find we are left with a story which is not even close to what really happened.

For anyone caring to research the text called The Missing Books of the Bible, they will be able to read how the baby Jesus was put on the back of a donkey to change it into a boy after an evil sorceress had changed the boy into a donkey! Or they can read about how the young Jesus "struck down dead other children who refused to play properly"!

No, Jesus was nothing like Saul had intended to portray him. He was a dynamic, forceful, and courageous man who was willing to place his own life on the line to teach others about the dangerous teachings of the priest craft. He definitely was not one "to turn the other cheek"!

Saul, however, chose to present Jesus as he did purely in an attempt to make personal gain. While the actions of Saul led Jesus to condemnation, he brought to himself fame, praise, and wealth. He created many of the fantastic concepts by taking actual events and then adding to them.

Such was the case of his account of Jesus' birth. He taught that Jesus was born in a manger over which a giant star appeared and shone. This led three Magi to him. Although three Magi did seek him out, this account is fantastic to any analytical mind. This star didn't just sparkle in space; it didn't even shine down on just Bethlehem. This was a star which "beamed" down on one small shed! And even more surprising is the fact these three Magi, living in Persia, more than a thousand miles away, were able to get there in just a few hours!

There are many accounts available which give a more accurate observation of what really happened two thousand years ago, such as The True Life of Jesus of Nazareth: The Confessions of St. Paul by Alexander Smyth, released in 1899 by the Progressive Thinker Publishing House.

This was successfully squashed at that time by the established Church. However it found life again in 1968, being published by Unarius Publishing. Other books which also offer confirmation to the following text of this book would be, My 2000 Year Psychic Memory: Mary of Bethany--Thirteenth Disciple to Jesus of Nazareth by Ruth Norman.

Another would be, <u>The Little Red Box</u>, an account which shows Jesus almost did become "King of the Jews"! But the most dynamic resource of all is a manuscript which was written by an Essene Brother of Jesus!

The Essene Brother wrote this account a few years after the public crucifixion of Jesus to an Elder Brother in Alexandria to inform the Order in Egypt about the circumstances which surrounded his friend, Jesus.

This written account convinced the Essenes in Alexandria that Jesus was truly a member of their Order. He was so rich in the secrets and in science and because he used their orders, customs, and recognition signs, they could not believe he would have practiced magic openly. Also, it should be pointed out that as was their custom, "an Essene spoke and wrote only the truth"! So only the strictest truth was ever written. Because of this, the contents of the ancient parchment have been placed beyond doubt. Part of this account, <u>On the Right Manner of the Life and Death of Jesus</u>, was also published by Unarius.

This whole world is a school. We have been sent here to learn. The concept of religion is that it is here to assist and guide us. If some religious teachings seem to lack any reasoning behind them, then we can assume they are only an embellishment added by Saul or one of those who followed him.

Every once in a while we must clean out our closets and get rid of the things which are useless to us. If something doesn't serve our needs, then we must make room for the things which do.

While scholars are tied up in debates about irrational teachings, we should place our attention beyond these petty fights. For once we look beyond our superstitious beliefs, we may find the truth is actually far better and far more important than the things we previously believed.

Also in this account, dialogue is not presented in an Old English format for quite obvious reasons. Jesus did not speak Old English or any other kind of English. Thus, translations have been presented in a simple and clear manner.

Part 1
The Beginning

Herod Antipas and Glaphira, the Princess of Iturea

During the reign of Ceasar Augustus, Judea was found to be under extremely harsh rule. In addition to the heavy hand of the Roman Empire, the people had much to fear from their own king, the one called Herod the Great.

While Herod had at one time proven to be a great king, building not only many temples but also complete cities, in his declining years he had become wracked with ill health and mental deterioration. He had become highly suspicious of all people about him and had even put members of his own family to death.

Shortly after Herod had his sister and his eldest son put to death for "causing disharmony in the royal family," even Augustus remarked it was better to be Herod's hog than Herod's son.

Herod had four sons, Antipater, Alexander, Aristobulus, and Herod Antipas, but it was only the youngest, his namesake, to whom he had ever shown any devotion, and it was Herod Antipas he made Tetrarch of Galilee, Perea, and Iturea.

Herod's choice was not due to Antipas's great wisdom or to his dedication to his father. The youngest son was much like the man Herod had become--selfish, uncaring, and devoid of any of the compassion needed to become a great king.

Antipas would often display bad judgment, and this was shown in his constant entanglement in compromising situations. He was known to have an eye for all comely women, and it made little difference to him about the results which might arise from any of these encounters.

One of the conquests he sought was Glaphira, the princess of Iturea, and although she did not appear threatening, he would be quick to discover she was just as cunning as he and quite his equal in seeking to serve her own desires.

In his attempt to seduce her, he had presented her with a small, jeweled, velvet-lined box which held two bracelets, both of which were marked with the seal of the royal family. His explanation was that these bracelets, one for him and the other for her, were to mark their undying love and devotion to one another. However this devotion was short-lived after he had successfully seduced her. Departing on the next morning, he left both bracelets behind.

Less than two months later, he received a message from Glaphira informing him she was carrying his child.

With her eye on the throne, she noted she should be by his side. She also commented on the health of King Herod and with his intent for Antipas to sit upon the throne, she should be made his wife before the birth of the child.

This message only served to anger Antipas, and he vowed to ignore her completely.

Glaphira was not one to be ignored, though. Just like Antipas, she had become used to having her way. She also sent messages to Herod informing him that since her child was of pure royal lineage on both sides, he was duty bound to recognize this child as his true grandchild and if it should happen to be a boy, he should be considered as an heir to the throne.

In addition, she sent a message to the Magoi Brotherhood, who were better known as Magi, or the "Wise Men" of the East. They were contacted by her so they might offer their assistance in having her child recognized, thus offering a foundation to the child's true heritage.

The Magi were men of notability, being not only wise men but also priests and highly respected astrologers who made their home in Babylon and Persia.

With her contacting them in the early stages of her pregnancy, they decided it might provide them with adequate time to prepare for a journey to witness the birth of this most notable child, as they had read in the heavens a most spectacular event was about to happen.

The Magi chose three among them to make the journey of a thousand miles, but they realized that with making the necessary preparations and making the actual journey, the endeavor would take many months to accomplish.

The Birth of a Prince

The many messages to Antipas had gone ignored and finally, with the birth of a boy child, she became quite adamant and fiery in her demand her son not be robbed of his royal heritage. She insisted it was God's great plan to have their son one day sit on the throne of Judea, becoming "the King of all Jews."

She could hardly be expected to realize the potential danger in which she had placed herself, never once considering Herod would attempt to kill any of his own blood, since the murder of his sister and son would not come about for many months yet.

With each message Herod received, he became more and more enraged. This was the third message from Glaphira, and he was now insane with anger. The second message had clearly laid out her intentions of her child being heir to Herod's throne if it should be a boy and now, in the third, she began to make demands on both Herod and Antipas.

Herod so greatly hated Glaphira he devised a plan to do away with both her and her son. This he carried out by calling on one of his most trusted officers. He ordered Caliph, the captain of his guards, to take two men and travel to Iturea to kill this firstborn, as well as the child's mother.

Caliph was informed that when one of the women of the palace was ready to deliver, they would be moved to the general women's quarters where they usually stayed with the child for up to three days.

The three soldiers arrived at the temple in the middle of the night. Caliph left one man as guard while he and the other soldier stole into the women's quarters. They quietly made their way to the nursery but upon arriving, were surprised to find two newborn babies.

Unknown to Herod or the soldiers, there were two other women who resided in the temple who had also given birth at almost the same time as Glaphira. And it was due to this lack of privacy that Glaphira decided to return to her own quarters with her child.

However, with Caliph finding two children, he was certain one of them had to be the child they were to kill. They drew their swords and slew both babies.

Next they entered the sleeping chamber, and again were confronted with the sleeping bodies of two women. Again, not knowing which might be Glaphira, they killed both.

While they were withdrawing, the nursery maiden awoke. To make sure there would be no witness to this act, Caliph slew her also.

What was intended to be a quick and simple act had now turned into a bloodbath.

In the morning, Caliph reported to Herod that his problem had been solved.

The Magi Arrive

The horrendous discovery in the morning gave light to Glaphira the depths to which Herod was prepared to go in preventing her from becoming queen.

She quickly gathered what she could carry, her child, and one highly trusted handmaiden, and they literally ran for their lives. Glaphira realized it would not take Herod long to discover his assassins had botched the job and they would be sent back to complete the task.

When the Magi arrived, they ventured first to the temple of Herod, knowing the child they were investigating was Herod's grandson.

Herod, believing that Glaphira was dead, welcomed the Magi with open arms and informed them they would find "the love of his life" with his mother in Iturea. He also requested they return to him before they departed. Under the guise of seeking an astrological reading, he was eager to get a full account of how well the event there was carried out.

More than a day had passed by the time the Magi arrived at the temple in Iturea. There they were informed some men had entered the temple and attempted to kill the princess and her child, but Glaphira had managed to elude the killers, although no one knew for certain to where Glaphira had fled.

Instantly, the Magi came to the conclusion perhaps the soldiers of Herod had rescued her and returned the two of them back to his palace. So they journeyed again to Herod to see if the child had reached safety.

Of course, when they related the events to him, he realized that contrary to the assassins' report, Glaphira still lived.

He informed the Magi he had no knowledge as to their location, but that he was most worried about the two of them and instructed the Magi to notify him immediately if they were to locate her. They agreed and left.

Joseph and Mary

Throughout the day, Glaphira and her handmaiden hurried along the road, trembling each time they heard hooves beating against the dirt road from behind, knowing it would be only a matter of time before Herod's soldiers would have them.

As night drew near, Glaphira finally realized that their deaths were most evident. If not this night, then most certainly by the next day. It was at this point that perhaps for the first time in her life, Glaphira thought of another instead of just herself.

It was the handmaiden's suggestion to pass the child to someone who might be trusted, who would be heading in the opposite direction. Soldiers would not be looking for a child who was heading south, back toward Jerusalem. But who would she be able to trust from all of the travelers who passed them?

Over and over again, the handmaiden tearfully reminded Glaphira they should not hesitate too long, for death could be only moments away.

Finally Glaphira saw an old man approaching, leading a donkey upon which a young, beautiful girl sat. Glaphira demanded that her servant approach and quiz them.

The servant stopped them and spoke at length. After a considerable time, she motioned for Glaphira to approach with the baby.

Glaphira also spoke with them for several minutes, explaining how the two of them would probably never see the light of another day and their only intent was to save the life of this innocent child.

There was great reluctance on the part of the man to become involved, but his heart softened when his young wife agreed the child should and could be saved by them.

At this point, Glaphira offered them the complete story of who she was and why she was being sought out. She also informed them they would have to remain silent for all of their days about who this child was, for she realized Herod might continue the search for the baby even after she had been killed. Then, in conclusion, she gave to the young woman the velvet jeweled box which held one of the bracelets with the marking of the royal seal upon it, as well as a document testifying to the true identity and heritage of the child. She asked only that the young girl let the child know, when he became a man, of the events of that night and how his mother was able to give him up only because she loved him so much.

The young girl solemnly agreed.

Joseph and Mary watched Glaphira and her servant until they disappeared into the setting shadows of night. They offered a prayer for the two of them and then set off again for their destination of Bethlehem, just south of Jerusalem.

Joseph and Mary were making the long journey from Nazareth to comply with the census law which required all males to register in the village where they had been born.

The Magi Journey to Bethlehem

Knowing Glaphira was cunning, Herod held back on sending any soldiers after her. Realizing the Magi were looking for her, he felt confident they would inform him when she was located. After all, there had been no indication that he was at the core of the botched attempt and there was still the possibility Glaphira might seek Antipas's assistance.

The Magi were easily identified by their robes, headgear, and other articles of clothing. So it was really no surprise Glaphira made herself visible to them as their camels loped along the road. It was at this point in encountering Glaphira they were finally informed about the full impact of the events and were warned to not let Herod know the child was being hidden amongst strangers.

She then offered what information she had, which was hardly more than her baby was with an old man and a young girl heading for Bethlehem with a donkey.

Meanwhile, due to the great crowds and the lateness of the day, Joseph and Mary realized they would need to spend the night in Bethlehem. It would be the next day before he would be able to properly register. After that, they would be able to begin their journey back home to Nazareth.

Joseph had brought sufficient coins to procure a proper room for them, but was quick to find there was no space available on this evening, even in private residences.

At the inn, Joseph explained that shelter was especially needed because his wife was with a newborn child. Finally the inn keeper suggested they might be able to make a bed in the stable. He informed them that while it smelled, it did offer shelter and some degree of privacy.

It was at this same time the Magi had arrived and carefully studied all of the people, looking for an old man and a young girl with a newborn.

In such a small place as Bethlehem, it was hardly any time before they located Joseph and Mary. They quickly realized there was a strong possibility they might take shelter in some form of lean-to.

As the three well-dressed men approached Mary and began to ask about the newborn child, terror filled her heart. She quickly informed them this was her child as she held him close to her bosom.

The three Magi smiled at one another. They had finally found the newborn king, but they knew they must let events run their course. They would not reveal they knew who the child really was.

They simply stated they wished to give gifts to her newborn, which they did, and then they disappeared almost as quickly as they had appeared.

Mary remained terrified throughout the night, fearing these strange men might lead the soldiers back to them. It was not until the next afternoon when Joseph was able to complete his duty that they finally, with a great sigh of relief, quickly departed and headed back home.

Part 2
The Young Jesus

A Boy Named Jose

Just as in the case of most small villages, talk and opinions flowed freely in Nazareth. Some old women asked, "How is it that the short time they were gone, they have returned with an infant and say it is their own? She was not even with child when they left and I know of no child who can develop that fast! Also, look--have you noticed they feed young Jose with goat's milk and not the milk of his mother?"

Surrounded by a great air of mystery, many jested that he most assuredly must be some sort of miracle child.

Once when Mary was asked by a nosy old woman where she had gotten this child, Mary answered simply, "From God."

"Undoubtedly," the old woman remarked.

Even though their son failed to resemble either one of them, the talk didn't bother Joseph or Mary. They knew if they just continued to live their lives in a normal fashion, the talk would finally end, and they were right. The excitement of issuing accusations eventually loses its appeal if those who are being targeted show little interest or care about what is being said.

Joseph was a carpenter and repairman of great renown and on many occasions would be found working in Herod's palace. As Jose grew older and began to show some aptitude in his father's trade, he would often accompany his father.

Although Mary protested he was tempting the fates by taking Jose to the palace, Joseph insisted it would look far more suspicious if he didn't take his son with him.

It was due to this exposure that Jose became deeply interested in spiritual matters and was often found to be upset about one matter or another in regards to the laws and practices laid down by the Sanhedrim. He often mentioned to his parents and to his friends that he considered them to be a bunch of hypocritical frauds who were attempting to control the masses with foolish embellishments and superstitions. It was from these opinions, formed at such a tender age, he would seek to destroy the Sanhedrim later in his life.

The Hermit Awakens the Power

When Jose reached his sixteenth birthday, he approached his mother and asked if she would finally agree to let him go to visit the wise man who was known as the "Hermit" who lived in a distant and almost inaccessible area of land.

Just as in the case of all mothers, she was reluctant, worrying about his welfare.

"But, Mother," Jose pleaded, "I'm not going alone. My cousin John will accompany me. We are no longer the two little boys out playing in the puddles. We are now men and need to be regarded as such."

Receiving a smiling nod from Joseph, Mary finally agreed and after making preparations, the two young adventurers were finally off on their great pilgrimage.

After a couple of days of attempting to locate the hermit with no success, they were on the verge of heading back home. Then just as Jose was about to give in, John began to yell wildly and motioned for Jose to climb up to the rocky shelf on which he stood. Climbing up, he was able to see a crude hut located below them on the other side. Wondering if this might be the journey's end, they yelled to the old man who sat outside, and they approached him.

By the time they made their way to his door, they were sure by his appearance that this was most assuredly the one they had been seeking. This was further reinforced by his statement, "I've been waiting for you. What has taken you so long to reach me?"

The three sat on the ground outside of the hut and spoke for several hours about many spiritual matters. They were filled with joy and wonder at the wonderful subjects about which he so freely spoke. These were subjects which would normally be spoken only in whispers among the closest of friends. Finally, here was someone who was not afraid of the foolish teachings of the priests.

As night slowly closed in around them, the hermit invited the two boys in to share an evening meal, and they happily accepted.

A Sign of Things to Come

As they ate, conversation eventually turned to the topic of "seeing." The old hermit denied being able to see the future since, as he had told them, there is no such a thing as a definite future: there is only a probable future and even that can be changed in just one second of time.

But he also informed them there were certain things which did come to him when he concentrated on them. "I can tell you some limited things about yourself, if you like," he said, "but mark this, boys--be sure you want to know the truth, for I will never lie while I am using this gift of God. Do you really want to know what I might see?"

"Of course," both boys echoed in unison.

"We didn't come here for lies," John interjected. "We want to know only the truth! What can you tell me about myself?"

The old man studied him for several minutes, then as he placed his palm on John's forehead, he said, "You have a great zeal! It is an overwhelming force which may eventually take over your mind completely! Unfortunately, it may be far more than you are able to safely digest into your aura. There are many things which point to your being a fanatic. This seems to be coupled with incorrect thinking. All of this shows you are becoming dangerously unbalanced. I see you living in tragedy, becoming badly unhinged, and possibly coming to a disastrous end."

John's face was spread with shock. This was not at all what he expected to hear. The hermit then looked into Jose's eyes, asking if he still wanted to hear what might be found out about himself. Jose paused for a moment, then slowly nodded his head.

Again, the old man stared at Jose for several minutes, then placed his palm to his forehead, and closed his eyes. "I see some kind of great majestic impulse but I cannot say I fully understand it. In your karmetic pattern, it appears you should have been some kind of king or great ruler, but that does not necessarily mean it will happen, only that you have the ability within yourself. But just as important, I see a latent power which is asleep at the base of your spine. While this is rare, it is not totally unknown among miracle workers. If this power were to be brought to life within you, you would be able to perform limited cures."

"Limited cures?" Jose asked. "Can you awaken this power?"

The old man admitted he could only try, then he motioned for Jose to join him outside, leaving John to sit by the fire, angrily muttering to himself.

The old man moved his hands up and down the sides of Jose, making sure he made the sweeping motion over the entire length, from his feet to the top of his head. This he did over and over again for more than fifteen minutes. Then, without speaking, he motioned for Jose to approach John to see if he could console him.

Without him being aware, Jose was performing his first cure in what would become a lifetime of curing.

Jose sat before John and asked him to look into his eyes. When John did so, he felt a wonderful flow of energy which passed throughout his body. He once again felt a great joy in his heart. However, it was at this point the hermit's warning began to show itself.

Suddenly, to the shock of Jose and the hermit, John began to acclaim great and strange things. "You are delivered from the Most High! The will of God has been shown to me! You are the one who the prophets speak of!" And with that, John passed into a deep sleep from which he would not recover until the morning dawned.

"Your cousin is a most unusual person," the hermit told Jose, and Jose was quick to agree.

On the next morning, after offering their thanks to the hermit, the two boys began their journey back home.

As they walked along, Jose explained to John that what he had experienced was due to a natural power and he never again wanted to hear him say things like he said the night before. John, however, being a natural fanatic, completely disregarded what Jose was saying. "I have always suspected there was something different about you! I heard those stories about how your parents left their home for a short time and then returned mere days later with this strange son! I have seen how people look at you and it is you that has taught me so much about spiritual matters. I know this is the beginning of your great mission!"

This only angered Jose all the more and eventually he gave up trying to talk to him.

By the time they returned home, their parents could see a great change had come between them. Jose refused to speak to or see John. Meanwhile, John would tell fancy stories about Jose to all who would listen, including a story about how the "evil one" followed them on their journey, but could not overcome them due to the powers Jose had.

Unfortunately for Jose, his love was so great for the people that he performed some limited cures, but this only served to give validity to John's outrageous claims.

Soon people were traveling great distances to seek his assistance. And with each cure, John became all the more convinced this was the one who had been spoken of; the one who would bring revolt and change.

Eventually Jose's cousin became so unbalanced Jose decided he would no longer associate with him; however, this decision lasted for only four years.

Part 3
Jose Becomes Jesus

Saul and Judas

Saul of Tarsus was the son of a wealthy tent maker, but when his father died he decided he would like to set out for an adventure. While the life of being a tent maker paid extremely well, it offered virtually no excitement.

He quickly converted all of his property into cash. The only asset he kept was the bond of a man who had become deeply indebted to his father. So as Saul went forth, he was found to be in the company of the man called Judas.

Although Saul was quick to realize an opportunity to gain a few coins when the occasion arose, he didn't really have any particular plan set in place as he entered Galilee. However when he heard stories from various individuals about a wild man who lived in the wilderness and proclaimed that a great warrior king was to soon lead all people to salvation, he was convinced this was some form of con to separate the people from their coins, and he was not above trying to figure out how he might be able to also take advantage of the situation.

When the next baptizing by John took place, both Saul and Judas were found to be among those who had come to watch.

While Jose was never seen in the company of John, he did finally agree to go to the river to be baptized only because his mother had begged him to do so. She felt tremendous pain for her sister's circumstance of having a son who had become so totally unbalanced. John now only wore rags and lived in a cave.

Mary asked her son to do this one thing for his cousin, perhaps with the chance he could talk some sense into him. Her reasoning was Jose could explain to John that by agreeing to be baptized, it would show he was a regular man.

While John was performing the baptisms, Jose walked into the water and approached him. John's face filled with joy at the sight of his cousin.

Jose quickly explained he was agreeing to be baptized to prove that if one were truly pure, they would not need to be baptized. His being placed below the water would prove he was no different than any other person.

After John lowered and raised Jose, he looked into his eyes and informed him, "It is now, with this baptism, that you shall no longer be known as Jose, but you shall now be known as the Chosen One, the Christos, the Savior of the downtrodden. Behold, you are now known as Jesus."

Then, just as fate would have it, there was a flash of lightning and a loud clap of thunder. John's eyes grew wide and he became all the more convinced his long-time suspicions were true. He began to dance around in the water and proclaimed, "Behold, the true Son of God is among us! Even Jehovah recognizes his son!"

The eyes of Jesus narrowed in anger as he told John, "I told you to no longer speak in this manner! With such foolish talk, you not only endanger my life, but the lives of my parents as well! Bother not to seek me out any further! Your actions are not only a danger to yourself, but also to all of those who are unfortunate enough to come near you!"

John continued to sing praises to Jesus as if he had not heard one word. Jesus turned and quickly left.

Saul and Judas, hearing only the praises which were being sung, turned to one another smiling. They were quite sure they were watching the groundwork for a clever con.

Jesus, The Liberator

While Jesus continued to deny he had been sent by God to deliver liberation through the sword, he did speak freely of the great injustices being carried out by the priests. From the days he had spent among them, he had become appalled at how they attempted to control the people, holding them in a grip of fear with false teachings.

The wrath directed toward him really had nothing at all to do with John's insane ramblings nor was it due to any Roman intervention. The truth was the Roman government had no concern about his lectures. He was definitely no threat to them.

His sole enemy was the Sanhedrim, and that was due to his denouncing the teachings of Moses. Jesus was against any tradition which attempted to control the people, and he openly disclaimed Jehovah, saying this was a false god. He proclaimed that things like anger, vengeance, jealousy, and the such belonged only to the lowest classes of man and no true god would have such vicious emotions. He also denounced blood sacrifices, pointing out that a true god would be associated with love and never with a blood feast.

To the Sanhedrim it was bad enough that any would speak out against Moses, but to have a man running about denouncing Jehovah and sacrifices was far too much. While they would tug at their beards, pulling out some of the hairs, in defense of the great Jehovah, they were probably more concerned with his talk about their sacrifices. They not only made a tidy profit from the sale of animals, but they would later feast on these sacrifices.

The teachings of Jesus made such great sense that large groups of people were beginning to reevaluate all they had been taught all of their lives.

Judas Approaches Jesus

As Saul began to learn more about this man who was now known as Jesus, he began to develop a clever plan. He informed Judas to follow this man and attempt to join his circle of friends and, if possible, be accepted as a follower.

Judas approached Jesus and informed him that he was greatly moved by the words he spoke and he desired to be one of his assistants.

After studying Judas for a short time, Jesus finally agreed to accept him and made him custodian and steward over all affairs of buying and selling. Judas was to be in charge of all worldly matters, which would leave Jesus free to concentrate completely on his ministry of awakening people to the fact they were all the true sons and daughters of God.

When Judas returned to Saul, he related his extreme good luck. They were only hoping to get close to Jesus, but they had never expected that Judas would actually be in charge of the money which was received.

Saul said he had developed a plan which would make the people quickly give up their coins to Judas, but the two of them would need the help of a third person. He said they would need the assistance of one who could prove to be as clever as he might be deceiving; one who was also a great actor.

Judas instantly knew of a man. He had grown up with just such a cunning and calculating individual.

Cosbi was the type of man who lived only for the day. He had no concern about any consequences or worry about tomorrow. He thought of religion as a folly in which the Sanhedrim showed they only cared for themselves and sincerely felt they really had no concern for others.

When Judas sought him out in Galilee and related the plan to him, Cosbi's eyes grew wide and he roared with laughter. Here was a chance for him to make some money, have fun, and make fools of the Sanhedrim all at the same time.

The plan called for Cosbi to use his talent to draw attention to Jesus, to show he was the true Messiah, and to prove he would free the people from all of their miseries. In turn, the people would offer their support and what money they had to prove their devotion to the Savior.

Meanwhile, Judas himself would be the one responsible for receiving the donations, since Jesus had made it perfectly clear he was not the least bit interested in monetary matters.

Cosbi informed Judas he could play the part of being a beggar to being a high priest, and Judas informed him that just a beggar would be sufficient.

"Although my new master is of good heart," Judas informed him, "he is fast to defame himself. People will not contribute to one who does not glorify himself! So the three of us need to spread his fame. For while it is true he can perform great healings, little will come of it if he keeps it hidden in modesty. But now, with your assistance, we shall magnify this and bring it to the attention of distant people."

"And give the Sanhedrim a fit at the same time!" Cosbi beamed.

Jesus Discovers His Heritage

Jesus traveled in wide circles and to distant places, but finally a messenger was able to locate him and informed him he should return to Nazareth because his mother was very sick.

Upon his return, he found his mother in very serious condition. At first, he held hope he might be able to bring a cure to her, but eventually lapsed into dismay when he found laying his hands on her forehead brought no response.

Mary opened her eyes and smiled at the son that she loved so much. "There is something I need to tell you," she said softly, pointing toward a pillow on a nearby couch. "Beneath that pillow...bring me the jeweled box hidden there."

As he moved the pillow and brought her the velvet-lined box, she continued, "We have always loved you with every ounce of our strength, but we have kept a secret from you! Now is the time I must tell the complete story to you."

Together, they opened the box and she explained the contents to him and related the story of how they had acquired him.

At first, he was greatly upset by this information, but he quickly regained himself for the sake of his mother.

He continued to sit by her side, holding her hand as she finally lapsed back into sleep. He sat there with her into the long hours of the night until she departed from her physical body. Even realizing she was gone, he continued to hold her hand. He continued to sit motionless even until the first rays of the sun began to shine into the room. Then he put his head to hers and wept.

Part 4
The Ministry Advances

Jesus' Attitude Hardens

Several days passed, during which Jesus buried his mother and entered into a state of mourning.

During this time, he refused to be seen by anyone. By the time he returned to offering instruction to the masses, they were able to see a new and more profound fire in his eyes and in his words.

On the Sabbath, he gathered with a crowd at the synagogue. Nearly all of the villagers were present and many had even traveled from great distances in the surrounding countryside, coming out of curiosity to see this man who so openly proclaimed such strange teachings. It had been made known that Jesus would address them after the morning service.

At the conclusion of the service, as was the custom, the rabbi announced that anyone desiring to speak or ask a question was at liberty to do so.

Jesus stood and mounted the rostrum. The rabbi asked Jesus from which book he desired to read, but Jesus quickly informed him he did not need these books.

It became as silent as death. Jesus gazed at them for a few moments, then began to speak.

"The prophet Isaiah said the Spirit of the Lord was upon him. Brethren, I do not presume to have even a guess as to what the prophet meant when he made that declaration. But I will attempt to address you from my own inner light.

"In the first place, this declaration must not be taken in a literal sense. What is meant by the Spirit of the Lord? When I say Lord, I mean the great life-giving force of the universe--and not the absurd, irrational, vindictive being our forefathers gave us to worship under the name Jehovah.

"As the great God force exists within the vast universe, it issues forth a divine essence which diffuses through all material and spiritual nature. This is the true Spirit.

"The Spirit of the Lord is upon me because it has enabled me to preach the true light to it's children. Shall we find the true light in the books of the prophets? No, my brethren, those books contain no wisdom. They do not contain the least idea about Spirit, the creation of man, or man's true nature. Neither do they contain a code of wise laws teaching how to live purely, nor do they give a glimpse of the life hereafter.

"The prophets were very common, ignorant men--ignorant of those things which they pretended to prophesy. Examine the books, then you will find they represented a tyrannical figure, absurd, fickle, cruel, and ignorant. If such be the God Jehovah, as they have portrayed him, what are they themselves? The greater part of them were cunning impostors. Some were fanatical zealots, others were madmen, and all were gloomy minded and desperately ignorant.

"Let me, humble as I am, enlighten your understanding as to what the true riches of life are. Let me aid you in finding the divine spark of immortal life, the divine soul which lives within you.

"Ever since our people have been led from slavery, they have been held in mental slavery under the dominion of a vile and selfish priesthood. Yes, brethren, your minds are locked up within the bounds of destructive superstition. You are barred by this priesthood from receiving the true light. When you look past their lies, you will then learn the fact the creator of man is not Jehovah, the God of the Jews, but the true God of the endless universes. You will one day see and feel the true source of creation and you will understand we all are divine sparks from the divine force. We all will ultimately lay claim to being the true sons of God!"

At this point, Jesus was prevented from continuing due to a great clamor which arose among the congregation.

Jesus descended from the rostrum and quietly approached the rabbi, who was violently hurling charges at Jesus. As Jesus approached, a sudden silence spread across the synagogue.

"What do you intend to do?" Jesus asked.

"I expose and denounce you as an impostor, a liar, and blasphemer," screamed the rabbi with increased rage. "You have blasphemed in denying our great God Jehovah, denouncing all of our prophets as impostors, and spoken vilely of our holy priesthood--and you are only the son of a carpenter, but you have the audacity to represent yourself as the son of God!"

"I said all of us are the sons of God," said Jesus calmly. "But not the sons of Jehovah, who is a false god, but the sons of the true life-giving force. Do you dispute my words?"

"I do!" the rabbi screamed.

"Then I will show you the power of the true God force," Jesus returned sternly. "And I call upon all of my brethren present to witness."

As Jesus looked into the rabbi's eyes, he stretched out his hands, one to each side of the rabbi's head. Then slowly, he moved his hands in a circular motion and then drew them gently downward.

The rabbi jumped as though he had received a sudden shock. His arms fell to his sides and his eyes closed. He seemed to be sleeping while still standing.

Jesus told him to open his eyes and to return to the rostrum. The rabbi obeyed, seeming to be unconscious of all that was going on around him.

Not a sound was heard or a movement seen as the entire congregation looked on in breathless astonishment.

Jesus spoke in a loud voice, saying, "Rabbi, the Spirit of the true God has now entered you so that you can now see truth and know the things I now know. Speak to these, my brethren, and tell them of my true heritage, as I have shared with your unconscious mind."

Then the rabbi, in a solemn and distinct voice, said, "Jesus of Nazareth is not the son of Joseph and Mary. He was born into the royal family--and just as you and I, he has shown me we are all the children of the true God! We are all the sons of God! And

Jehovah is a tool used by the priests only to control you!"

"Now, my brethren," said Jesus, addressing the people, "bear testimony of this man's words to you!"

Jesus then waved his hands toward the rabbi, who again became his natural self as Jesus departed. The people rushed to the rabbi to question him on what had just happened, but he said he had no memory of it. He insisted it had been some sort of trick manifested by the evil one and this man, Jesus, was his emissary.

The rabbi became even more enraged than before and he soon collected a small party from the congregation, and they rushed after Jesus. Catching up to him, they grabbed him while screaming and lifted him off of his feet. They hurried through the village to the southern end where a ravine was located.

As they approached the ravine with the full intent of throwing Jesus over the edge, four rough-looking men armed with clubs rushed to his defense. They began swinging their clubs violently and within the first blows, eight were laid out with serious injuries. The remainder of the party, seized by terror, fled and left Jesus unharmed.

Two of the rescuers took charge of Jesus and hurried him away. One of these was John of Galilee, and the other was John's brother, James. The other two rescuers were Judas and Cosbi. The latter two brought up the rear to make sure there would be no more such attacks on Jesus.

The Apostles

As Judas spent more and more time with Jesus, he became even more confused by the actions and decisions of this man. He seemed to take no action to protect himself, even though there was a threat of violence coming from those who were frightened by his radical teachings.

These people had been taught their entire lives to fear and love Jehovah. Now a man walked among them who dared to speak against Jehovah. While some believed him to be a god, just as many thought him to be a fool. Then there were those who sided with the rabbi, insisting he most assuredly was the evil one.

Also, Judas noted Jesus surrounded himself with characters of very low morals who were barely much better than those Jesus had spoken against. Judas looked upon the closest comrades of Jesus as base, dull, and greedy. To him, there was no difference between them, except one would be less cunning than another.

Word had spread that he not only could perform cures and limited miracles, but he had claim to royal heritage, so it was not strange that some men of greed would attempt to attach themselves to him, hoping they might collect big when Jesus made his final move--whatever that move might be.

Jesus accepted many with the intent to assist them in becoming teachers so they could better offset the sway the Sanhedrim held over the people, but the entire objective of this lowly group was based on what each might gain. Judas knew they would follow Jesus only as long as there was the prospect of gaining fame, fortune, or political power. Beyond that, he saw them only as deserters once they might believe their desires could not be achieved.

Jesus, having completed a sermon on the plain of Genesareth teaching the people they were divine sparks and not just merely a body they saw in a reflection, agreed to give healing to all in need. Standing aside, he permitted Peter, whose former name was Simon, to announce the event.

In a loud voice, Peter announced, "As the address of Jesus has finished, if there are any among us who are sick, if they will come forward, Jesus will relieve them by the laying on of hands."

There were about twenty sick people who gathered together when Jesus entered among them with Peter, Andrew, John, and James.

One by one they were cured and departed in a joyful manner, each having their pains removed.

Near the end, Judas made his appearance, pushing his way through the crowd followed by a miserable and unfortunate-looking man. His back was so bent that he arched forward, almost touching the ground with his hands. He wore only rags.

The beggar began to plead for help, asking Jesus to cure him of his most terrible condition.

Being he was escorted by Judas, Jesus looked at him inquiringly.

In a loud voice so that all might hear, Judas asked Jesus if he would heal this poor man who had heard of his powers.

"But Judas," Jesus replied in a distressed voice, "I am afraid I may not have such great an ability as to assist this poor, unfortunate man!"

"But Master," Judas insisted, "neither you nor I nor anyone else really knows the extent of your powers. It may be even greater than we think. Let us hope God will extend the power for the benefit of this poor man. Try, dear Master."

Jesus approached the deformed creature and passed his hands over his body several times.

When Judas gave a wink to the deformed man, he suddenly became erect and started bounding all around with a great burst of energy.

The multitude gasped in astonishment. Jesus as well as his followers were also surprised.

Jesus immediately emphasized that it was not he, but the Father within who could bring about such a miraculous event.

The man quickly bounded away before anyone had the opportunity to question him, quickly escorted by Judas.

Once they were fully out of sight of any of the others, both began to roar with laughter. "Oh, Cosbi! Cosbi! Did you see the looks on their faces? When you jumped up, I swear the whole group jumped at the same time! With the looks on their faces, it was all I could do to hold my laughter in!"

"Oh, God!" Cosbi exclaimed. "That was great fun! And now they'll have enough to keep them excited for a month!"

Judas quickly returned to the crowd alone and began to walk among them with an open money pouch, and the coins poured in.

When Judas reported back to Saul about how well things went, Saul was quite excited also. He became even more excited when Judas opened his pouch and displayed a fair number of coins.

Saul began to walk around the room, engaged in deep thought. "This can be even bigger than we previously thought. Why should we be pleased with a mere handful of coins when we can even compete with the Sanhedrim? This man does have powers! And with our assistance, perhaps we can make this bigger than all of us! But now the only threat I can conceive would be from his close circle of friends. Will they be any threat to us, or could they help serve us?"

Judas smiled. "You don't need to worry the least about them! They are fools, braggarts, and dull-minded! They are dedicated to nothing but their own greed. And as for any of them helping us, their greed is only matched by their lack of talent! Although they can't be trusted by Jesus, they certainly can't be trusted by us either. I'm sure Jesus will finally see their true colors before much longer anyway.

"Of the party, first there is young John of Galilee. Thinking he could gain an advantage in life, he ran away from his father to join Jesus. Then there is John's brother, James. We picked him up in Nazareth where he had come to seek John by his father's orders. These young men, along with their father, Zebedee, are very ignorant and silly, but yet very selfish. I told them of Jesus' true heritage and that eventually he might become the King of Judea. In turn, they wanted to help Jesus with his work, with the understanding they might become governors of their own province and would gain great wealth.

"The next is Simon, whom Jesus calls Peter. This man is a merry, good-hearted fellow, possibly the most intelligent of the group. He is generous and could not stoop to do any mean thing, however, he is with us mostly due to his desire to gain power also.

"Then there is that ignorant, awkward, selfish brute, Andrew, brother to Peter. Also, there is Nathaniel and Philip, both of whom are two more miserable, ignorant, and sordid creatures who joined us. These two were so poor they were willing to believe anything, say anything, and do anything for the slightest prospect of a reward.

"It seems that Jesus just doesn't have the ability to see the true nature of a man, so I'm sure there will be others coming along who won't be any better than this sorry bunch!"

"He couldn't even see through you!" Saul laughed.

A look of pain appeared on the face of Judas. It was true he was deceiving Jesus, but in his own heart, and unknown to Saul, Judas had developed a true feeling of love for Jesus. Had he not been bound to Saul, more than likely he would have been the one true follower. He knew he was the one man in the whole world who would not betray Jesus.

Part 5
Other Miracles

The Fish and Loaves

People throughout the land were beginning to hear of the miracles of Jesus and most believed their Messiah was among them. As members of the group traveled about, telling their tales of the Great One who would soon be coming to teach them, expectations grew to a zenith. So did the stories about Jesus.

Passing through many towns and villages, Jesus gave addresses and performed some cures as he went along. The men of the group would relate about many things which had happened before--and most would add to the account. At one point, Peter told the story about the power of Jesus' love.

In the original account, Jesus was giving a sermon to about forty or fifty people when he stopped so they could eat their midday meal. He quickly noted only half of the people brought something to eat. He made mention about brotherly love and how if each person brought food would share with one who did not, then perhaps all might have something to eat.

Those with food shared with those who had none and found they had more than enough.

The first couple of times Peter told the story, it was pretty accurate, but Peter felt it lacked an exciting element; one which would impress the small villages. On the next telling of the story, he told how there was close to a hundred people and Jesus fed them all, paying for the food from his own money.

This story also quickly changed. He then said there were close to a thousand people and five hundred loaves with two hundred fish supplied by Jesus.

The next place, he said there were three thousand people, one hundred loaves, and fifty fish.

The story then changed to being five thousand people, ten loaves, and five small fish. Then he claimed there were six thousand people, five loaves, and only two small fish, and all were fed from that.

Finally, Judas had to suggest to Peter that he not reduce the number of loaves and fish any further or they might begin to think he was telling one of his fish stories. However, the final account Peter settled on was there were six thousand people, five loaves of bread, and two small fish--and once everyone had eaten their fill, there were still twelve baskets full left over!

The Casting of Demons

When the group left Galilee and returned to the other side of the mountains, they decided to visit a village called Gadara. This was a village built on a cleft in the side of a mountain and inhabited by Gentiles who raised swine.

These were people of a very simple nature and were extremely superstitious. They believed sickness and madness were caused by demons who had entered the body. It was due to this that Judas and Cosbi thought of another plan.

After the group, led by Jesus, crossed the lake and began to ascend the mountain, many of the villagers came halfway down the narrow path to greet them.

The path was not only narrow, but steep, and the swine were allowed to roam about as they pleased.

There were caves located near the spot where the two groups met and as they began to exchange greetings, a monstrous-looking man came out of a cave. He rushed among the people, causing them to flee in terror.

He stood in front of Jesus in torn garments, waving a large club as he announced, "Be gone! I know who you are! You are Jesus of Nazareth. You were sent by God to drive the demons from me, but I will not let them go! For I am the demons!"

Jesus looked at him with an expression of bewilderment.

Judas, knowing this was another of Cosbi's disguises, asked Jesus if there was any possibility this man's reasoning might be restored.

Jesus looked into the man's eyes and stretched his hands out to him slowly. After a few motions, he uttered, "Peace to you, dear brother."

The madman continued to wave his club, but now with less energy and enthusiasm and finally he fell to the ground.

Jesus again approached him and for several minutes ran his hands up and down his body.

After a few minutes, the villagers returned again and watched in total amazement.

Slowly the man opened his eyes, looked about, and remarked about how well he felt. He jumped up and humbly bowed to Jesus, then burst into tears. With that, many of the villagers drew close to the madman, no longer fearing him.

Cosbi then began leaping for joy, but as he went too near the edge of the road, he accidentally slipped off and dropped down on top of some swine that were at a lower level. The swine, receiving so sudden a shock from such a horrible-looking beast, ran off as fast as they could. Many jumped over the cliff and were killed. Others made it to the bottom of the mountain and rushed out into the lake where many more were drowned.

A few days later, the fame of Jesus was spread even further among the people. Now they heard stories about how he had driven the demons out of a madman, cast the demons into swine, and then commanded the swine to kill themselves.

As the story grew, so too did the exaggerations about the event, but this was usually from the people who had not been there and knew no better.

After the adventure at Gadara, the group was joined by two more followers. One was Matthew, who possessed the rare talent of knowing how to read and write, but was noted for being a great babbler of absurd stories and monstrous fiction. The other was Thomas, a disagreeable atheist who believed in nothing which didn't contribute to his own personal needs.

Part 6
True Events

Jesus in the Temple

On Passover, Jesus had chosen to give one of his discourses on the front steps of the marble structure which had been dedicated to Jehovah. Here again, he took the opportunity to denounce the concept of a vicious and distrustful god.

"If the god of Moses were a wise god," Jesus began, "he would not have needed to enter into a contest of wills against the Pharaoh. If he chose for our people to be free, he would not have hardened the heart of the Pharaoh. If this was a true god, would he have needed to provide force against an unyielding will? Here, then, we may perceive that the statement is not a fact, or the Lord is inconsistent and cruel. We have a tale of the greatest inconsistency and absurdity which has ever been related. Either the tale is one of the grossest, lying, absurd productions, or Jehovah is an absurd, cruel, imbecile monstrosity.

"You may then perceive, my friends, that the history of the exodus is not a reliable fact on which the Passover is founded and the god Jehovah, if he had anything to do with that affair, is not worthy of our thanks, our gratitude, or our notice.

"If you wish to believe in a wise and powerful God and wish to obtain his favor, why do you make a monster of him by making these disgusting offerings to him? Do you think a good and wise god can be pleased with the greasy smoke which ascends from the altar this day? Is your god nothing more than a monstrous, gluttonous animal that will devour these dead carcasses along with the blood which has been set aside for him?

"No, my brethren, such a thing cannot be possible. You are mistaken in what the true God who presides over you is. You have been worshipping a figment of your imagination, encouraged by a wicked priesthood. And this handsome landing where I now lift my voice, instead of being a place devoted to learning, has become a den fit only for thieves and money grabbers."

The address of Jesus was suddenly discontinued when shouting arose among the people. "The profaners of the temple! The thieves! The money changers! Down with the money changers!"

Judas quickly recognized the discontent was being caused by his friend, Cosbi, who now wore a patch over his eye and a hump under his clothing. He was waving a club and attempting to get others to follow him.

"Come, my brothers," he screamed. "Let us clear the temple of these profaners." Then he rushed forth, followed by many ruffians. Coming to one of the money stalls, they upset the tables and beat the changers until they fled, then there was a scramble for the money, which was soon scooped up.

Jesus attempted to stop the destruction, even grabbing some of the ruffians, but he was roughly pushed aside as even others began to join in. Soon all of the stalls were upset and robbed.

Jesus continued to attempt to stop the destruction and restore order, but he was held back by Judas and Peter.

The mass of people, seeing the illegal proceedings, quickly left in fear. Jesus was dragged along with them by his two escorts. They knew the soldiers would be there in no time at all.

Cosbi, seeing the Roman guards approaching, dropped the patch from his eye, pulled down the hump, and made his escape without being recognized as being the originator of the disturbance.

Lazarus and Mary

Strange as it may seem, one of the greatest enemies of Jesus was Saul, but this was not due to any hatred for him. Quite the opposite was the case. Saul had great admiration for Jesus, but it would be his actions and decisions which would prove most disastrous for the man of love.

Jesus not only gave the people the most complete code of morals, but he gave them the most sublime ideals of man's inward self. He gave glimpses of the nature of the soul and the great God of the universe as not taught in Jewish theology.

Saul saw these doctrines of Jesus as pure truth and he realized he was not doing him justice by substituting silly fables in place of the golden teachings. Through Saul, Judas, and Cosbi, Jesus had been converted into a myth of unnatural and impossible origin, but yet it was these fables which kept the purse of Judas full, which in turn, gave sustenance to himself.

Saul, just as Judas, saw the bulk of the followers as being greedy traitors, and deep in his heart he realized Judas possibly cared more for Jesus than any of the others might.

Strangely enough, one of Saul's biggest fears was these followers might turn against Jesus too soon. There were many plans still being formulated and they were still very instrumental in these plans.

Many had begun to complain their expectations had not been met. They felt they had been deceived and at the first opportunity, confronted Judas, demanding their wages. Judas endeavored to pacify them, but that only made them more angry, raising their voices, making threats.

Jesus entered during this occasion and looked at Judas with an inquiring look. Judas and the rest were taken by surprise at his appearance and most were ashamed he witnessed such a disgraceful scene.

Although Judas was tempted to inform Jesus about the type of men they were, he realized this was not the time to break up the company. He quickly took the entire blame on himself, saying he had thoughtlessly overlooked their needs.

When Jesus asked how much money was in the bag, he was surprised to find Judas had collected one hundred and fifty shekels of silver.

"Who knew so much money existed in the entire countryside?" Jesus remarked. He then had Judas give ten shekels to each member of the group. This was a slight setback for Judas, but one deemed necessary for the time being.

As the shekels were passed out, a messenger from Bethany arrived. After Jesus read the note, he announced his friend Lazarus was sick and his family requested his immediate attention.

Now being in a better frame of mind, the group agreed to travel there with him.

As they reached the home of Lazarus, they were met by Martha, his eldest daughter. Weeping, she informed them her father was dead.

"Dead!" Jesus exclaimed in astonishment. Motioning for Martha and the others to wait, he entered the chamber of mourning. Mary, the youngest daughter, rose from her seat and threw her arms around his shoulders and burst into tears. "Oh, my beloved," Mary cried, "if you had been here, he would not have died!"

He held her for several moments, then led her gently back to her seat. Jesus then advanced to the bed, removed the cloth, and studied the body for several minutes.

He noticed the corpse didn't display any of the features of death. The body was not cold, but actually quite warm. Also, there was no odor and he looked like he was simply asleep.

When he touched the face, he noticed it was soft, and when he touched the eyelid, Jesus let out a cry of surprise.

The visitors looked at each other in alarm. Jesus noted the eyelid quivered at the touch and he could see a quivering at the corner of the mouth. "Lazarus lives! He has not left the body!"

Looks of amazement spread around the room as Jesus frantically attempted to revive Lazarus. When Lazarus let out a slight groan, many fled the house in terror. Outside, Judas and the others stood in shock.

Very little was known about the human system in the days of Jesus. Many aspects were not known about at all. All serious conditions were said to be caused by demons, and when one became cured, it was taken for granted that the demon had been cast out. The state of a coma was often mistaken for death.

Although Jesus did not know the nature of this particular incident, he had learned other men had experienced similar conditions. With the recovery of Lazarus, most fled to the safety of their homes.

Jesus and his group stayed for the night to show there was nothing to fear. However, before the sun rose high in the sky on the next day, the news had spread all over Jerusalem that Jesus had raised Lazarus from the dead.

Mary, the Thirteenth Disciple

It was common knowledge among the group that Jesus was deeply in love with Lazarus's youngest daughter, Mary. Jesus had not even tried to hide the fact that on many of his visits to Bethany, the journey was made solely to see her.

This was of little concern to any until he told his group that Mary would be a member, often traveling with him as he spread his words across the countryside. This outraged everyone except Judas. They frowned on the thought of a woman being escalated to the same status as they. But there was even more of a reason for their wanting Jesus to have nothing to do with her. Just as Judas, she easily saw through each of them, knowing what was truly in their hearts. Although she made no attempt to hurt Jesus with this, she did let each of them know how she felt.

The men who were now looked upon as the disciples of Jesus proved how deceptive they could be. Many remembered a time when a prostitute was about to be stoned to death and Jesus intervened to save her, telling the people to let one who was without sin cast the first stone. Although this woman had been forgotten about, with none remembering her name--if, indeed, they had even known her name--they now referred to her as Mary with the strong insinuation that this beloved of Jesus was that same prostitute.

As they wandered about the countryside, telling the many stories of Jesus, this fable joined the others in the telling.

Judas, on the other hand, tried to end the lie, often telling people where he went that this Mary was as pure at heart as was Master Jesus himself. This served little purpose, though. People were always more interested in some deep, dark secret than in hearing the truth.

Judas sincerely felt sad about this since he knew she was his one true disciple. She loved him with all of her heart and he knew she would be there by his side when the end came--whatever that end might be.

Part 7
Confronting the Priests

The Feast of the Tabernacles

Knowing that Jesus would attend the Feast of the Tabernacles, held on the grounds of the Holy Temple, Judas and Cosbi devised another plan to tease and torment the Sanhedrim.

As Jesus passed among the people, many begged for him to place his hands upon them. Others were content just to touch him. Some desired only to touch his robe, for they believed this would bring peace into their troubled worlds.

He gratified many by touching them. Then a blind man was led to Jesus. "Master," pleaded the blind man, "have pity on me. I have been blind my entire life. I was born blind, but I have faith that you can bring sight to me."

Jesus looked at him sadly and informed him that since he had never had sight, this was a matter for God.

The blind man still continued to beg for mercy, until Jesus finally relented and informed him he would do all he could, but the man should understand that if anything in the least came of this, it was due to the intervention of the ultimate God force and Spirit, and not from himself.

Jesus then carefully touched his eyelids with the tips of his fingers and concentrated.

A silence spread among all of the people in attendance as they watched for the anticipated outcome.

After Jesus withdrew his hands, there was an extremely long pause. Finally, the man let out a tremendous shout of astonishment. "Praise be to God and Jesus of Nazareth! I can see! I can see! Praise Jesus, I can see!"

Judas told the blind man's friends they needed to get him home as fast as possible so the bright sun wouldn't destroy his new sight.

Before the man left, though, Judas gave him a huge hug and whispered into his ear, "That was great, Cosbi! This is the best one yet! Simply great!" With that, Cosbi and his two comrades made a hasty retreat.

When Jesus returned to his walk, a group of scribes and pharisees approached him and with a scorching tone of voice, the superior asked Jesus, "We wish to know by what power you do these things! Is it by our Lord God Jehovah or by Beelzebub, the evil one?"

With that question, the pharisees smiled at one another. The superior felt he had Jesus trapped. Since Jesus had denounced Jehovah, the only god the people had ever known, he would surely have to admit he served the evil one or recant on his statement about their Lord.

Jesus regarded the question with contempt, but gave an answer. "I will ask a question of you and if you answer mine, I will answer yours. By what power do you conduct yourself?"

The superior scribe quickly answered all of his actions were through the power of God.

"Exactly," Jesus answered, "just as it is with us all. All that I do is in accord with the divine plans of Spirit, and especially so within the temple."

The superior quickly countered, "And by what authority do you speak? Perhaps it is the evil one himself who says these things through you! Perhaps he is also responsible for your so-called miracles! Wouldn't the evil one do fantastic miracles, seeing that they could advance his cause?"

Jesus looked firmly into his eyes. "All that you can see is due to the light of the sun. You know your world through this light. Meanwhile, Spirit is the sun of my world and all that I see within me comes from this light of Spirit."

"This is blasphemy!" the superior exclaimed. "This doctrine of yours comes from the arch fiend himself!"

Jesus addressed the whole body of scribes and pharisees. "It seems you will denounce me before the tribunal of the Sanhedrim for stating the truth about myself. What will you do if I testify against you? You sit on the seats of the high tribunal established by Moses as the rulers of the people of Israel, but there is no truth within you!

"You wish to blind the people and make fools of them. You impose heavy burdens of taxes, of offerings and presents so you can live a life of laziness! How long will you be the pest of the nation? Indeed, in my serious judgment, a mad dog is more worthy to be called rabbi than such conceited, puffed-up set of hypocrites as you are."

The scribes and pharisees broke into a dreadful demonstration, shouting, pulling their beards, spitting at Jesus, and hissing at him through their teeth. They would have sprung on him except for the fear of what the crowd might do.

Judas and several others surrounded him for protection, then they quickly led him away.

Jesus realized he had placed himself in great danger and took the advice of his friends and remained in seclusion for several days.

Caiaphas

Saul, by this time, had carried his overall plan to an even greater elevation. He realized Jesus could be killed at any time by any of the many fanatics who surrounded the priesthood. At first this thought distressed him, fearing that would cause the loss of the tidy sum coming to him on a regular basis, but after he thought on the matter for a while, he realized that more could come from this than just receiving mere coins.

Now that the people were becoming convinced Jesus was the Messiah who would lead them to freedom, Saul sought to establish his own basis for a religion. Seeing that the people were dedicated to spiritual subjects which had become immortalized, he could see that the same could be done in the name of Jesus.

Saul knew Jesus was at his zenith of fame and popularity. From this point, it could only fall apart, whether it be due to the people questioning the fables which were being told, the disciples leaving him, or Jesus being confronted with a healing he couldn't perform.

One of the duties Judas carried out under Saul's orders was to keep the hopeless cases away from Jesus. He had once asked Judas, "What if he can't make the truly blind see? What if someone asks Jesus to raise their dead child who has only recently died? What if Jesus fails in any of a hundred different things which could happen?" Saul had begun to realize it was time to go into his final stage of planning.

Saul began to work closely with Caiaphas, the head priest. He was even the one who would carefully lay out the stages where Jesus might be executed. Thus Caiaphas placed an injunction forbidding anyone to interfere in any matters which related to Jesus so that they should not spoil the deeply laid conspiracy against him.

Saul, addressing the priests, informed them, "I lay before you a plan I think will meet your satisfaction.

"As you have been made aware, this man Jesus is of royal heritage. While I have not seen the documents for myself, my servant Judas has. Jesus keeps these documents, which are a claim to the throne, in a red velvet box.

"Will Jesus finally make an attempt to one day sit on the throne? Who knows? But I do know Antipas is his father--and I do know Antipas sits on the throne! But how would such a thing affect you?"

He took a long pause to make an effect. They knew of Jesus' tremendous hatred for them.

"While he has done nothing but bring attack against you, how much worse could he make your life by sitting on the throne? In my plan, it will be necessary to bring him within the grasp of the controlling Romans.

"I have made him a very popular man all over Judea and Galilee. Now for anyone to be popular and not be a Roman is almost equal to the death sentence. It will take very little to make the Romans believe he is also their enemy.

"Having accomplished this much, I have had Judas persuade Jesus to return to Jerusalem. Since he has made mention of his royal heritage, when he arrives there, we intend to hail him as King of Judea, the temporal and spiritual king as was promised by the prophets. I shall also employ some people to tempt him to say disrespectful things about the Roman Emperor. If we succeed in this respect, perhaps they may take him then. If they don't, it won't matter. We will still be able to make our case afterwards. We will arouse the anger of the Romans one way or another.

"Once we can make him speak against Rome, you will have sufficient grounds to take Jesus as your prisoner and turn him over to the Roman governor."

Treachery on All Sides

Several days after Jesus' visit to the temple, he realized his life could be in dire danger, and he also realized he could not depend on his many friends to save him since they were mostly from the poor class and weak in comparison to his enemies.

His friends sent word to him, advising to not come to the city if he valued his safety. He therefore resolved to make the house of Lazarus his home until something could be decided among his group. But there was another reason to not travel to Jerusalem. There was the desire for his own earthly bliss. He even thought to himself that perhaps the time was right to resign from his labors and settle down in domestic happiness with Mary.

This prospect frightened the apostles, though. They were still certain Jesus would one day sit on the throne, but they had no intention of letting this thirteenth disciple, this Mary of Bethany become queen. This was another reason they had begun to spread the rumor Mary had been a prostitute. They knew the people would not tolerate having a whore sit on the throne with him.

Being of a keen mind, Mary felt something was going on and when in the presence of the company, she whispered in his ear, "Beware of traitors in this company. Do not go to Jerusalem."

Later, while walking through the garden with Mary, the two of them heard Peter on the other side of the hedge speaking against him. He suggested to the others that perhaps they had made a mistake in following Jesus. The sudden understanding of things filled Jesus with sadness and alarm. Now he understood the warning of Mary that there were traitors in the company, and this caused him to cast an eye of distrust on all around him. This made him all the more sure now was the time to abandon his teachings and to forsake going to Jerusalem.

When Jesus confided this information to Judas, he quickly hurried to let Saul in on the news.

Saul became greatly distressed. Jesus would have to carry through with the plans if Saul's goal was to be reached. He immediately contacted Caiaphas, and together they prepared a letter stating they were preparing to take him prisoner from the house of Lazarus because of the things he had said on the temple grounds, but through their love of Jehovah, they would agree to drop charges if he would leave for Jerusalem. They also said another condition was he never speak again against the Sanhedrim or against the Roman government. In either case, they could reopen charges and have him arrested.

When Jesus received the letter, it met favorably with the company, but not with Jesus. His mind had been made up that this was the end of his work. He then asked Judas what he thought, since Judas was of a sharper wit and mind than the rest. When Judas finally said he agreed with the others that he should go, it was only then that Jesus sent word to Caiaphas and gave his word they would depart.

Part 8
The Trap Is Set

Jesus Enters Jerusalem

Under Caiaphas' supervision, the great scheme was laid out and a tremendous amount of money was spent to recruit a sizable group who would pretend to be the followers of Jesus.

Jesus and the disciples made their way down the mountain road to Jerusalem, but once they arrived at the base and then finally made their way across the arched bridge, they found a large number of people assembled.

Jesus was surprised to find more than two dozen children had also joined the great assemblage and each of the children held a palm frond they were waving in his honor.

Two of the smallest children greeted Jesus at the bridge, and they held a rope which was tied around the neck of a donkey which they held up to him, offering it so that he might ride the animal into the city.

Saul knew the habits of Jesus well enough to know he would decline the offer to ride from anyone except possibly a small child.

Although he didn't desire to exalt himself in such a manner, he smiled at the two innocent children and mounted it. Then the group continued on their way with Jesus in the lead, riding the donkey led by the two children, while the other children sang praises of welcome to the new king of Jerusalem.

Hearing these words, his face suddenly turned sullen. He realized he might very well be sliding into a trap.

While the children sang and the adults cheered him on, Caiaphas knew enough to not make a large spectacle of the event before they actually entered the city's gate. If the guards should turn them back, fearing Jesus was a troublemaker, their entire effort would have been in vain.

Once Jesus arrived at the gate, two of the guards stepped forward and challenged Jesus and his group, wanting to know their intentions. Jesus quickly assured them they were coming only for celebration and had no intention of causing any revelry.

Asking if Jesus would be responsible for the actions of each and every member of the group, he quickly agreed, although he looked about and also wondered what their true intentions might be.

A short distance inside the city, he was to discover that a much larger group of people had assembled, many of whom were singing praises. "Glory! Glory! Praise be to the king of kings! Jesus our Savior has come among us!" His face filled with grave concern.

Jesus slid off the back of the beast and slowly made his way to the steps of the temple. He walked up the steps only high enough so that all could see and hear him. He always took precautions to never presume he was more superior to any by placing himself on a higher level than those he was addressing.

He began to speak about brotherly love, but was almost immediately interrupted by one of the paid men. "Praise be to you, Lord! Tell us again, are you the son of God, or are you the one and only true God?"

Jesus' eyes narrowed as he gazed at the man and then at his own disciples, wondering if any of them might be in on this plan, especially since they had all been so intent on him making this journey.

"No," he said with a glare, "I am not God and I am the son of God only in the same sense that you are a son of God!"

"Then you are saying you are the son of God?" he yelled back, trying to wear Jesus down.

"As I said, only in the same sense you are the son of God. God is not something strange and foreign to us. God and Spirit are one. We each are sparks from the great fire of God and Spirit gives us our life! But I am not something that you are not! You, too, are a divine spark from God, just as yonder Roman guards are also!"

A murmur broke out among the crowd, and another man opened with an attack for fear they might lose the group over to him. "Lord, what do you think about the Romans?"

"They have given much to this city," he said in all sincerity. "They have helped us build fine roads, brought sanitation to not only Jerusalem but also the small villages, have developed great strides in our agriculture--and let us not forget they have tremendously lowered the element of crime."

Another cried out, "Then you are saying it is all right for us to be the slaves of the Romans?"

Jesus let out a sigh, feeling far too tired to engage in a war of words. His thoughts returned to his beloved Mary, and now he only wished he had not permitted the others to decide his fate for him. At this moment, his dominant desire was to walk away, but again he countered the attack. "Reach into your pocket and take out a coin."

The man was a little confused but eventually did as Jesus requested.

"Now tell me," Jesus asked, "what image is on that coin?"

Looking at the coin, he answered, "Caesar Augustus."

"Then I would say the coin belongs to the Romans for this was created by the Romans and marked by the Romans. Meanwhile, the human soul belongs to God. So I say to you, give to Caesar that which belongs to Caesar and give to God that which belongs to God."

Another man began to push his way to the front of the crowd. Jesus recognized him as being one of the scribes with whom he had had a run-in at an earlier date.

"You give us fancy words," the scribe yelled out. "You carefully dance around instead of trying to answer our serious questions! We want to know your true feelings about our Roman masters! What are you? Are you a god? Are you a king? Or are you merely a mouse that roars? Do not give us trick answers! Answer us directly as a man!"

Jesus looked down at two of the disciples who stood in front of him and in a low voice he said to them, "If this is what you desire, then this is what you shall receive."

Feeling very alone, he cast all care to the wind as he proclaimed loudly, "You want to know my true feelings? Then I will share them with you! I know the Romans for what they are, treacherous and dangerous--but as treacherous or dangerous as they may be, they are all we deserve! We are not men! We have done nothing to improve our lives! But this I put at the feet of the priests! They have destroyed our great civilization with their superstitions, greed, and foolish teachings! We will never be free of our Roman masters, nor should we be until we have brought down these fat and lazy bloodsuckers!"

With that, he stepped down and began to walk back into the crowd. As he passed his disciples he said, "I hope I have pleased you," addressing none in particular.

The Red Velvet, Jeweled Box

Saul and Caiaphas were very pleased with the results of their endeavor. They knew charges could now be waged against Jesus for a multitude of reasons, but most important would be the charge of causing hostility against the governing rule. While the Roman government cared not about his attacks against the priesthood, they would have to bring him to task on his claim the government was dangerous and treacherous.

Saul felt there was one important element which might still spare Jesus, though. When Jesus would be presented with the full list of charges, one charge--that he could be the king of the Jews--would fall apart if he should decide it was time to finally display the legal documents which had been given to his stepmother shortly after his birth.

So Judas was sent back to Bethany, to the home of Jesus' beloved Mary, to retrieve these documents and the jeweled box in which they were kept.

Upon being greeted by Mary at the door, Judas informed her the trip to Jerusalem had been a trap and Jesus had sent him for the box, telling him it was time to make the documents known publicly.

At first Mary hesitated. Jesus had been very adamant about her protecting the box and not letting anyone take charge of it except for himself.

Judas continued to insist, though, stating Jesus was being held within the city walls and would not be permitted to leave while charges were being gathered against him.

Finally, Mary did realize that Jesus knew how she felt about all of the disciples except for Judas and Peter, and if he were to send someone, it would undoubtedly be one of these. She also reasoned that since they had previously both heard Peter's unkind remark, he probably would send Judas.

At length, even though Jesus had told her to not trust the contents to anyone, she did get it and slowly turned it over to Judas.

As he made the journey back to Jerusalem to meet with Saul and Caiaphas at the temple, his heart was very heavy with remorse. He knew he was helping to seal the doom of this man for whom he had great respect and love.

Upon entering the temple, he held the box to his side and when he encountered Saul, he still was not certain if he intended to hand this document over to be destroyed.

Noting his attitude, Saul told him, "Be of good cheer, my dear friend. You have been faithful and highly dedicated to me since my father's death. When this ordeal which is so upsetting to you is over, I will consider your bond paid--you will once again be your own man."

With this prospect, Judas handed over the box, then turned, lowered his head, and walked back outside.

Once Saul held the box, Caiaphas quickly grabbed it from his hands and opened it. After studying it for some time, expressing some amazement, he finally returned the document to the box, then entered into his private chamber with it. No one would ever see this box or its contents again.

Part 9
The Dye Is Cast

The Last Supper

Mary and her sister, Martha, had already intended to attend the feast that was planned, scheduled to take place the day after Jesus entered Jerusalem, but after receiving the disturbing news from Judas, they decided to leave immediately.

Late that same evening, the two of them arrived at the home of Simon, where Jesus was to spend the night and where they would hold the intended next day's feast.

Seeing each other, they ran to one another's arms, after which Jesus asked how it was that she had arrived a day early.

When she informed him she had learned about the plot against him from Judas, he looked at her inquiringly. "Judas? Judas returned to Bethany to tell you what happened here?"

"Yes, that and to retrieve your documents back to you," she sobbed. "He said you sent him to get them from me."

A strange expression filled Jesus' face; one which baffled her. But now the matter of events were becoming more and more clear to him. Just as if he had stepped out from a darkened room into the light of day, he found himself now stepping out from the darkness which had clouded his mind into the light of reasoning.

"How clearly I am beginning to see things, my love! I never sent Judas!"

Her face filled with fear. "Surely you don't suspect Judas has turned against you? Have you seen him yet? I'm certain he'll turn the box over to you the very moment he sees you!"

"I'm sure you are right," he said in a voice which displayed more doubt than Mary cared to hear.

Judas did not return to Simon's home that evening nor during the course of the next day, until it was time for the meal.

Meanwhile, Jesus knew the Sanhedrim would be wasting no time in preparing official charges against him.

During the next day, Jesus dedicated his whole day to Mary, knowing this would possibly be their last time together. Neither made mention of Judas or the jeweled box. Nothing would be said at this most precious time to mar their deep feelings.

It was not until after the others had gathered that Judas finally made his appearance.

While his entrance was little noted by most as they stood in small groups, making conversation and partaking of wine, Mary saw him and quickly rushed to his side. Jesus, on the other hand, looked at him, but remained seated.

"Do you have the documents with you?" Mary asked in a low but excited tone.

His eyes fell on Jesus and never looking away, he answered, "Yes, yes, of course."

He moved slowly to Jesus. Coming to his side, he stood rigid and uneasy. Although their eyes stayed locked, neither spoke for some time.

"Mary has told you I have your documents?" Judas finally asked. Jesus slowly nodded. "They are safe, master. I didn't bring them with me for fear the soldiers might be here. I will have them for you later."

Jesus continued to look deep into his eyes, much the same way he did when he first agreed to make Judas his steward. However, the look now was much different from the one he had given him at that time. Judas was well aware Jesus had the ability to read what was in one's heart--when he chose to take such a look.

Judas slowly sat next to him. "I want you to know that none has loved you like I have!" Judas blurted out.

Jesus refrained from making a remark, but motioned for the others to take a seat.

Slowly, Jesus addressed them. "My beloved friends and brethren, the hour has at length come in which it is my sorrowful task to tell you that this will be our last time together.

"I have endeavored to enlighten humanity on the nature of God and to inform them Jehovah was a false understanding of the true higher spiritual existence. I have endeavored to show them they possess immortal souls which come directly from God's own divine essence. I have taught a code of morals and I have shown them death is nonexistent, that life continues on a much higher level. This and much more have I attempted to teach. But when there is a controlling factor which chooses to thrive on lies, then we find that truth can be dangerous to those who expound it." He then continued to speak about the darkness of the heart, wherever that darkness may be found, whether in the hearts of the priests or in the hearts of those who may be much closer to you, even in the hearts of those who you love deeply.

Listening to his words, several hung their heads in shame. He then made mention that there were some at this table that would betray him. That statement brought a round of denial, several yelling out, "Not I, master!"

Contrary to Saul's later account, he did not single any out, but instead offered them his love, saying that although he might die for the sins of some, he loved them still and he forgave them.

Hearing these words, Judas began to rise.

"Where are you going, Judas?" Jesus asked as he held his arm.

"I am going to get your documents, master."

Jesus again looked deep into his eyes. Seeing a tremendous pain, he slowly turned him loose as he remarked, "Go to them! Seek out the priests and do what you must!"

Judas, with a very surprised look, quickly left. He wondered to himself how long Jesus had known the truth.

Judas at the Temple

Judas entered the temple quarters seeking to meet with Caiaphas, but met resistance from the minor scribes insisting that it was far too late for Caiaphas to be bothered with the likes of him.

His insistence became so loud that, eventually, Caiaphas's assistant and then Caiaphas himself appeared, demanding to know who was daring to cause such a commotion.

"It is I, Judas," he answered. "I must speak with you about the jeweled box! I must get it back from you!"

"The jeweled box?" Caiaphas asked. "And what jeweled box would that be?"

"The one that I brought to you and Saul. I must retrieve the documents which were inside!"

Caiaphas simply smiled and informed him he wasn't sure what he was speaking of, that he had no memory of any jeweled box nor of any documents.

Judas went from loud to becoming violent, charging toward Caiaphas. He was blocked by the assistant and grabbed by the two scribes. The palace guards also quickly rushed in.

As the guards began to remove him, Caiaphas motioned for them to wait. He left for his quarters and after a few minutes, returned with a gift.

"Judas," Caiaphas said as if in a loving nature, "know that you have done the work of Jehovah! Jehovah loves and smiles upon you! Not only have you served Saul well, but your cunning has served this temple. For this reason, I offer this payment to you."

He handed Judas a pouch filled with Roman coins, which Judas opened, looked at, and then after a pause, flung at the head of Caiaphas.

The guards dragged him to the entrance and threw him down the temple steps. At the bottom of the steps, Judas wept.

Mary and Jesus Retreat

At the base of Mount Olivet, on the north western side of Jerusalem, was a beautiful garden which was often frequented by inhabitants of the city because of its peaceful nature. Jesus had already made plans to escort Mary there on this special night, after their feast had concluded.

Ever since he had made the decision he would leave Bethany, he had set his mind to ending his ministry--and to proposing to Mary.

That was to be the happy ending for this most wonderful night, but although circumstances had changed, he still brought her here to testify his undying love for her. Some of the disciples, not fully understanding his intent, followed. At the garden, though, Jesus requested they be left alone, and the two of them journeyed deeper into the garden, while the group made themselves as comfortable as possible, sitting on the ground, discussing the new events.

Part 10
The Arrest

The Group's Last Decision

The official charges against Jesus of Nazareth had been filed with the clerk of the Roman court earlier in the day. This was then sent to the temple of Antipas Herod, as customary when an official hearing was being requested. It was at this same temple that Pontius Pilate, the fifth governor of Judea, would also sit in attendance when charges were being leveled against any individual or group, and this was especially the case when such charges involved serious discipline or matters of interest to Rome.

However, both the court and the temple were in agreement that they should attempt to avoid a disturbance between the followers of the Sanhedrim and the followers of Jesus. The arresting unit would not be sent out for him until darkness had fallen.

Judas became aware of this unit upon his return to Simon's home. The unit, learning of the intended feast at the home of Simon, went there. When they discovered the group had left, they took up positions nearby in the hope they would return again this same night.

It had been Judas's decision to confess fully to Jesus about all of the events which had transpired and to warn him to escape from Jerusalem. Seeing the guards, though, he also hid in the shadows to watch and wait.

On the far side of the city, in the garden, the group was now extremely upset by the sad turn of events.

Andrew made violent gestures and angry expressions as he addressed the others. "Our desires have not been fulfilled! Everything we attempted fell to trash! And now we have even lost his ear, with him listening to the wench! If she knows what is in our hearts or not, we surely know of her feelings toward us!"

"Take heart, Brother," Peter answered, as his thoughts seemed to be far away. "It doesn't really matter what comes from her whore mouth. The court will have him in their grasp shortly anyway."

The others began to mumble and grumble among themselves, wondering what was to become of them. They realized that regardless of past rights or wrongs, they were now just as poor as they had been when they first set out on this so-called adventure, but now, more important than that, was the question if they would even escape with their lives.

After a few more complaints were shared, the group, all except for Peter and Andrew, quickly left, seeking to hide somewhere that might be safe.

"You know," Peter continued to Andrew, "while the others will mark this up only as an experience, being quite content with just escaping with their skin, there may still be an opportunity to be made here! You remember the heavy pouch Judas always carried about? I'm quite sure Judas has made out extremely well in this matter!

"As for us, instead of choosing to follow another master, or worse yet, return to our miserable lives as fishermen, we should set out, becoming masters ourselves!"

Andrew's eyes lit up. "Collecting an easy living from those who have followed him! And there are now many more followers, both far and wide!"

"You are quick to pick up my intentions," Peter continued. "Let the others go. We have made a reputation for ourselves as we have traveled about. Most even already know our names! It will still be an opportunity for us to continue our travels, telling our grand and glorious stories, just as we have always done! And the coins will still continue to pour in, but the only difference is they will go into our pouches!"

"And of Judas?" Andrew asked.

"He is quite clever! Perhaps far more than we ever credited him! But instead of being in opposition to him, perhaps we could merge our talents with his! I have always suspected him of being at the base of many of the miracles we have seen! Perhaps he can help us stage further miracles!"

"But the biggest question of all," Andrew interrupted, "how do we, ourselves, avoid punishment and possibly even a sentence of death? After all, we have also been accused of being blasphemers!"

Peter looked sternly into Andrew's eyes. "The end of Jesus has come. There is no longer a need for us to stay with this boat which has sprung so many leaks. It is now time to separate ourselves from him completely. It matters not when the soldiers take him. The fact is they will find him, and they are going to find him soon! He knows this himself! And you know, as well as I, he will not attempt to flee! If they do not have him this evening, they will have him by tomorrow! It is time we now attempt to make allies with Rome!

"Return to the home of Simon. When the guards do make their appearance, whether it be tonight, tomorrow, or the next day, be there and attempt to convince them you and I will gladly be in service to them! Meanwhile, I will be like a shadow to him, following him wherever he may go, so we know of his location at all times. Together you and I will endear ourselves to both the court and the priests by turning Jesus over to them!"

Andrew nodded and was off quickly, returning to Simon's home.

The Encounter

Neither Judas nor the soldiers had long to wait. In less than an hour's time, Andrew was seen approaching Simon's home.

Instantly, the guards and their captain circled Andrew. "You are seeking the man called Jesus," Andrew said in a voice so loud Judas could hear from his distant, hidden spot. "He is in the garden of Gethsemane! Follow me and I will take you to the very spot!"

The captain seemed amazed at his eagerness to assist and felt there might be some deception at hand. He ordered Andrew to be held there as a prisoner by two of his soldiers while he led the rest of the detachment to the garden.

As the soldiers began to make their way, Judas hurried ahead. His dominant thought was perhaps he could at least spare Jesus from capture.

Arriving at the garden just minutes before the soldiers, he found Peter asleep with a flask of wine clutched closely to his chest.

Judas moved quickly down the path until he could make out two dark shadows which turned out to be Mary and Jesus.

"Master," he cried out, "you must flee! The soldiers are right behind me!"

Jesus gave a startled look, but remained by Mary's side. "Judas, you are an enigma to me. Of all, you have been the most difficult to figure out! Do you yourself know what is in your heart?"

"Master, I have loved you like no other disciple has done, except perhaps for your beloved Mary. If I only had time to let you know the horrible truth of why I was obliged to betray you! But now is the time for us to quickly depart!"

"I am going nowhere," Jesus answered calmly as he turned his attention to his beloved. "I want you to wear this bracelet for all time," he said softly as he placed the bracelet on her wrist. He had removed it from his red velvet box before he left for Jerusalem with the full intention of presenting it to Mary on this night with the request that she be his wife.

"This was the bracelet my birth mother gave to the only mother I have ever known. It was given to her the same night I was. It is the greatest gift I have to offer you. Through this bracelet, you are united into our grand circle of love! Know that no matter what happens, I will always be as close to you as this cherished bracelet!"

Judas could only drop his head and turn to give the couple their last few moments of privacy together.

In the distance, they could hear the heavy march of footsteps coming closer. Suddenly, though, two soldiers sprang from out of the bushes which circled them. These two had been sent ahead to trap the prey should he attempt to flee.

One proclaimed, "You, sir, known as Jesus of Nazareth, are under arrest!" He grabbed Jesus' arm, while the other soldier grabbed Judas.

Within moments the captain made his appearance, followed closely behind by two soldiers who held another prisoner between them, and then by the detachment of eight more soldiers.

Dragging the prisoner before Jesus, he could see it was Peter. The captain, addressing the prisoner, asked, "Do you know this man called Jesus?"

"No!" Peter proclaimed.

The officer shook him and asked again, "Take a good look. Do you know this man, Jesus?"

Again, without hesitation, Peter answered, "No! I told you! I don't know this man!"

The officer then directed his attention to Jesus. "We found this man asleep at the garden entrance. Can you identify him?"

Jesus remained silent for a few seconds, feeling completely betrayed. Even those who he loved dearly had now left his side. He could easily see the fragility of the human heart and wondered if perhaps he had wasted all of these years in endeavoring to raise the people to a spiritual nature.

"When you first approached me," Jesus finally answered, "I believed I knew him, but now I can see I was mistaken! I can honestly say I do not know this man and I have never known him!"

Peter remained silent, head hung down, refusing to look up at Jesus.

"And what of this one?" asked the soldier who was holding the arm of Judas.

"This one is known by the court," the officer answered. "He is of no threat. Obviously, he held the prisoner here so he wouldn't escape."

"Could I ask only one favor from you?" Jesus asked the captain. "Would you see to it this woman is escorted safely to her home? I can only ask this of you and your soldiers. As you can see, there are none here I can trust!"

The officer's attitude softened as he answered, "Yes, of course, sir!"

Jesus embraced Mary as she wept bitterly. One could even note that many of the soldiers were moved by the tenderness of the moment, watching as tears rolled down Jesus' cheeks.

Then, being allowed one final kiss, possibly for all time, the assemblage departed.

The Charges

In the palace of the Sanhedrim, located in the court of the temple, was a magnificent chamber which easily held the seventy members of the council. It was this seventy, led by their Nasi, or president, which ruled upon the laws of the faith.

When Jesus was dragged before them, it was the Nasi who would address him, informing him of charges and any decided outcome.

It was the middle of the next day when Jesus was led in, surrounded by officers of the court, with two more guards behind them.

The Nasi rose from his seat and proclaimed to his brothers in attendance that a great deal of blasphemy had been spread among God's chosen people and the accused was now even claiming to be the king of Israel.

Reading the official list of charges, he began, "First charge is this man Jesus has been heard to deny the divine authority of Moses, saying that much of our history is a lie!

"Second, this man Jesus has said the people of Israel are not a chosen people, but instead, are ignorant, wild, cruel, and savage!

"Third, this man Jesus has said Moses was a cunning impostor and all of his revelations were pretended and his intercourse with God on Mount Sinai was a lie!

"Fourth, this man Jesus has said our God Jehovah was a only a creation from out of the mind of Moses, and the attributes we allow to Jehovah were really based on the nature of Moses--which was stern, cruel, and ignorant!

"Fifth, that our Lord Jehovah, being of stated nature, is not worthy to be a God, not even a king, but is no better than the lowest of men, being filled with hate!

"Sixth, this Jesus asserts that Moses' accounts are nothing more than lies and fables. He has said the stories of our scriptures are nothing but absurd fiction and resemble no truth to our true history!

"Seventh, this Jesus has asserted our sacred Order of Priesthood was not ordained by any Lord or God; that we are not wise, pious, or learned. But instead he has accused us of being cunning knaves who are only interested in stealing from the people, keeping them enslaved in mental darkness!

"Eighth, this man Jesus openly asserts there is no such being as Jehovah! He has said the God spoken of in our scriptures is nothing more than fiction, created only to control the minds of ignorant men!

"Ninth, this Jesus then claims there is a greater force than our beloved Jehovah, who the people can call upon in spirit and truth!

"Tenth, this mere man then claims to be the son of some god! Moreover, he claims to be the king of Israel!"

After the charges were read, some witnesses were called to verify they had heard him speak these things, after which Jesus was permitted to speak.

The Charges Answered

Extending his arm toward his seventy judges, he addressed them in a bold voice.

"You men of Judah, who are self-styled sacred priests, hear my true words! It is not in defense that I address you, for I know that would do no good! You are not true judges, but actually only closed-minded bigots who care not for truth and seek only to secure your own positions in our society.

"What you have brought against me as charges are really only so many truths. The first eight charges can be answered by asking you, Is there anything in the character called Jehovah that any man of common sense can accept as divine nature? By examining this cruel being in the light of philosophical reason, we can easily see that Moses, with his limited knowledge, created this Jehovah, the god of only the Jews!

"Yes, all of this was from the mind and creation of Moses! Let us look at this Jehovah as he is represented by Moses. It is asserted that this god is all-powerful, all-wise, and all-benevolent. Now taking this into consideration, let us examine the works and holy scriptures.

"I have not blasphemed against any god, not even your Jehovah. Let us consider the account of the creation. Did Jehovah in the beginning create the heavens and earth out of nothing?

"Philosophy tells us there never was an atom of matter ever created or destroyed. Did he make the day before he made the sun, or even any of the billions of suns which might exist? Did he make the sun to rule the day and the moon to rule the night? That is impossible, for both are really only from the source of the sun. Did the Lord feel tired after working six days and then have to rest on the seventh? This account of the creation could not have come from a wise god, for it shows a great perversion of facts. This only shows these concepts came from the minds of ignorant men!

"I will pass over endless other ridiculous accounts which leave just as many important questions unanswered and would ask you about the Garden of Eden. In the Mosaical account, it states God saw everything was good, yet he planted a tree of evil to tempt and tease his children. The consequence was they did what he tempted them to do, not knowing any better in their innocent state. They sinned and displeased God. That is a most absurd and ridiculous statement, totally destructive to the loving nature with which you wish to present him.

"Would a wise and good father put temptation in the way of innocent children to tempt them to do wrong? No loving father would do this, but in this stupid account, he is shown to do even worse. He not only tempts his children to sin, but he curses them forever for falling into the snare he laid for them!

"As for Moses, we only have his own word about his discussion with God. Any reasoning man can easily see this account was a silly lie! Since he didn't know how to identify God, he used symbology the people could understand. He claimed he talked with God through a burning bush, and through this bush God said 'I Am That I Am'. Now Moses knew no more than he did before! This nonsensical statement is held even to this day as some divine conception of the Deity! This is nonsense because it does not convey an idea. Can it be opposed that if this god Jehovah wished to reveal himself to any mortal, he would have given such an indefinite description?

"Moses has said Jehovah was the God of Abraham, Isaac, and Jacob. However, a true God would have been the creator of all mankind and would have not made such a limited and foolish statement. He certainly would not be partial to any one race of people!

"The fact is there is no such being as the god Jehovah. He is a figment of the imagination invented by our ancestors, resembling their own natures. He was created in the image of themselves both in body and in mind, having the same passions as they. It is said God made man in his own image, which meant the inner self, the soul! But here they have represented their God as being exactly like themselves with eyes, nose, ears, and every other body part. If they had tails, then they would have undoubtedly given a tail to Jehovah! To this imaginary god, they gave all human passions including love; hatred; revenge; vindictiveness; cruelty; hope; fear; hesitation; doubt; sympathy; pain; pleasure; and a love of praise, flattery, and adulation! This god is no better than a mere mortal!

"That there is a great and wise power existing by which this vast expanse of universes are controlled and maintained is as true as the god of Moses is false!

"I have always said we are all the children of God, meaning each of us is a divine entity who has been given the opportunity to be placed in a particular physical body to help us learn more of the nature of the lower worlds.

"In this nature, I have said I am a son of God, but I have always been quick to reinforce that with the fact that includes every living being on this planet! Every man, woman, and child comes directly from this ultimate life force! We are never separated from the true God as you feel you may be separated from your Jehovah.

"As for the charges that I have claimed to be the one true Messiah, the Christos, or the redeemer of mankind, I have given no sanction or encouragement to these things and feel these open claims have been originated through the workings of my enemies.

"Now, men of Judah, my accusers and judges, I have made an end to my explanations that I have felt necessary to clarify. I do not ask for your pity or mercy, for I know such would be useless. I know you thirst for my blood and therefore patently await my doom, and let the blood be upon your heads!"

There was only a deathly silence among all seventy members as they sat in awe at the words and reasoning of this man. Suddenly, Caiaphas, fearing he was losing sway over the council, jumped up and tearing off his girdle and casting it out onto the floor, which was a sign of guilt, began to scream, "You have heard the defense of this blasphemer! He has denied Jehovah! He has denied the truth and wisdom of Moses! He has even denied our divine authority! What need do we have for further consideration? Is he worthy of death or not?"

Then the Nasi tore at his garment and cast it to the floor. Then a third sprang to his feet and followed the example of the previous two. Soon the entire seventy had removed their girdles and cast them with the others.

Although they had pronounced the death sentence on Jesus, they knew they would need to make a case before Pontius and Antipas, not having the power of life and death at their disposal.

Part 11
The Final Act

In the Palace

To the northeast of the Holy Temple was a magnificent palace which had been built by Herod the Great. It had a flight of marble steps which rose up to a stupendous terrace surrounded by numerous marble pillars. This was the entrance into the great Hall of State where two thrones could be found sitting on an even much higher elevation, which again, had marble steps leading up to them. It was here that Antipas and the governor of Judea would sit when such a ceremony was called for.

It was in the early afternoon of the next day that Jesus was led to this palace where Antipas and Pontius Pilate had agreed to be in attendance.

As Jesus looked up at the two men who would now sit in judgment of him, he was of mixed emotion. Strangely enough, he had never felt either of these great men were his enemies. In fact, in the back of his mind he even had the thought he was looking at the man who may have been his father, but he quickly subdued such a thought.

Looking at these two men in person for the first time, he noted how Pontius was a portly man of about middle age, but one who had an air of conscious power and dignity of station. He also could see that Antipas was a tall, slim man, seeming to be older than Pontius. He had a haughty and scornful expression. He was dressed in a purple robe which was decorated with figures made from gold, and he wore a golden diadem upon his head. Jesus was also surprised to find him adorned with numerous chains, bracelets, and rings.

On the right and left of the great chamber were detachments of Roman guards, and in front of them were a great number of Sanhedrim members. At first, Caiaphas and the Nasi were greatly pleased with how well things were going, but when Caiaphas noted how Pontius glanced at Jesus with an expression of compassion, he became uneasy.

Finally, Pontius addressed the Sanhedrim. "Reverend sires and ministers of Jehovah's Holy Temple, why do you bring this man before us?"

"Most gracious sir and mighty governor," the Nasi answered, "this man has been guilty of grossly insulting and blaspheming against our holy institution and the God we worship. He has been arraigned before our sacred tribunal, tried, and condemned, but as we have not the power to inflict punishment, we bring him before your honored sirs."

The eyes of Pontius hardened as he addressed the Nasi. "You may accuse a man for transgressing your sacred laws, try him, condemn him, and punish him to a certain extent, but you are not allowed to take his life. That is the property of the state!"

"That is not the reason we are asking for his death," the Nasi quickly responded. "We are not asking you to judge him about our sacred laws, but we seek for you to judge and condemn him on offenses committed against the state!"

"That would be another matter," Pontius agreed. "What are these charges?"

The Nasi unfolded the scroll and proceeded to read the charges they had prepared the night before.

"First, this man has spoken disrespectfully against our most illustrious and gracious emperor Tiberias many times, in many places.

"Second, he has denied the justice and lawfulness of paying tribute to the emperor.

"Third, he has denounced the Emperor as a tyrant and usurper of the rights of the Judean people.

"Fourth, he has endeavored to incite the people to rebellion against their rulers.

"Fifth, he has caused the eagle of the Romans to be treated with indignity.

"Sixth, he has proclaimed himself to be the rightful king of the Judean people and has endeavored to withdraw the allegiance of the people from their rulers. All of these charges we have witnesses to verify."

Pontius cast a suspicious glance over the members of the priesthood. He realized everything Jesus had ever said about them was probably very correct. They were not above deceit or corruption.

He was doubtful about the charges they were bringing against this man and from the start, intended to free him. But if anything of a treasonable nature could be proven, he was bound to see that all such offenders were strictly punished.

With reluctance, he gave the order to proceed.

Various members of the Sanhedrim stood forth and one after another gave statements which seemed to confirm Jesus' guilt.

Distressed, Pontius addressed Jesus. "Unfortunate man, what do you have to say in your defense?"

Jesus raised his eyes to the governor. "Your Highness may observe that my enemies have taken advantage of me. They knew I would not be prepared to answer the charges they now bring against me. All I can say is I am ignorant of these charges. I have never said or done that which they claim."

Pontius glanced at Antipas. It was quite evident to both that while Jesus may have been guilty of many things, nevertheless these charges were all puff with no substance.

Pontius again addressed Jesus, "Do you have friends who can bear testimony for you? Look around--is there any who can speak for you?"

"There are thousands in the city," Jesus replied. "All of them know what I have said, but as for personal friends, they have deserted me, as they are afraid of persecution from the same men who persecute me."

The captain of the guard left his position, moved beside Jesus, and informed Pontius that there was one friend who was not afraid to testify.

"And who would that be?" Pontius asked.

"It is I," the captain answered.

The priests shrank back in shock at this announcement, but the eyes of Pontius sparkled with delight. "Then speak, man. And do not be afraid to tell all you know. I want to hear all you have to say in his favor!"

"I simply wish to state the occurrences which led up to the arrest," the captain answered, "which I think will go far to disprove the charges brought against him."

The captain then told about the day Jesus arrived in Jerusalem. He spoke about how he was orderly and when Jesus saw a rebel attempt to disrupt the group with turmoil, he had asked a guard to arrest him. He then related how some had attempted to trick him into saying something against the Roman rule, but Jesus defended the government and even said many benefits had come from the Roman presence here.

"Then, by the gods, this man is innocent of the charges!" Pontius announced with great energy. "It is not necessary to continue this investigation! This man has done nothing to merit death!"

Caiaphas advanced in front of the governor. "I beg your Highness to consider that this man has been charged with treasonable designs. Yet you ignore the testimony of many and consider the words of only one man. Is this the course of Roman jurisprudence? I very much doubt it, so I shall object to this decision."

Pontius had never been friendly with the High Priest, but he knew Caiaphas had some favor and influence in Rome. He realized it would not be prudent to show any hostile feelings toward him. Therefore he attempted to curb his anger.

It was at this point Pontius decided to dissolve the tribunal to discuss the matter in private with Antipas.

Jesus was led back to his prison and the holy priesthood filed out, gathering in smaller groups outside until that time the governor and their king were prepared to reconvene.

The Second Encounter

Pontius and Antipas took a two-hour repast during which they ate and discussed at length what decision would be reached in regard to the victim. Antipas already knew Pontius's attitude toward the priests and how he desperately hated the idea he should be forced into doing their will.

Both of them were conscious of the fact Jesus had done nothing to merit so great a punishment, and Antipas even admitted he knew he had performed no evil to the state and the charges against him were probably nothing but lies.

"However," Antipas concluded, "I think your Highness should take my advice and give him to the priests. I know this high priest, Caiaphas, well enough to know he is treacherous and extremely dangerous! Should you offend him by refusing to condemn this Jesus to death, he will seek an opportunity to revenge himself on you! He has great influence with the emperor at Rome, which enabled him to be appointed to the high priesthood. I therefore advise you to keep friends with him by giving him this man."

Pontius was caught between two very difficult choices. On one hand, he could give in to the Sanhedrim, although he felt he would be humiliating himself by going against his own wisdom. Or he could possibly raise the wrath of the emperor by not taking all steps to preserve the peace. He realized Caiaphas would cause endless distress and turmoil if Jesus were to be freed. He also knew he would have to answer to the emperor about why he let things get out of hand, when such disturbances would break out.

After the two hours had passed, the priests once again began to assemble before the entrance to the Great Hall. Before they were permitted in, though, Pontius wanted to speak with Jesus in private.

Jesus was then brought before just the two of them and Pontius began to query him. "You poor unfortunate man. What is it you have done to make them hate you so much?"

"I know I have greatly offended them," Jesus said meekly, "but I have done nothing more than speak the truth."

"Truth!" exclaimed Pontius. "And just what is this truth?"

"Truth in regards to the ways of my accusers!" Jesus responded. "I have only laid open the wickedness of their hearts. That they display only meanness and ignorance. That they hold man in their control by subjecting him to endless fear. And that they are not only evil teachers, but blind guides as well! This is the truth I have spoken and is the truth for which they seek to destroy me."

"My God!" Pontius exclaimed. "It is no wonder they seek to destroy you! Truth is a very dangerous tool! Many a man has died for nothing more than speaking the truth! But my experience in life has shown me a man cannot prosper in society if he chooses to speak such truths." Turning to Antipas he asked, "What should we feel, my Lord, if the truth were spoken about the two of us?"

Antipas gave a large smile. "It is horrible to contemplate!"

Finally, Pontius gave the order to permit the accusers to enter. The members quickly assembled and eagerly awaited the decision.

Pontius viewed them with contempt and remarked to Antipas under his breath how their eyes looked like those of serpents. They reminded him very much of a snake pit, where the snakes were raised up, looking skyward, watching for their victim to fall into reach of their fangs.

"Most holy and merciful priesthood of the great God Jehovah," Pontius said in a bitter and sarcastic tone, "look upon the man for whose blood you so greatly thirst! It is with great reluctance that I turn this man over to you! Without my making accusations to you, I would ask that you look into your own hearts, if you are able, to see if you are truly each a better man than he! If you can do this with all sincerity to the God Jehovah, then you may put him to death. If, on the other hand, you should regain clarity of mind, and desire to show how merciful priests are, you may exile him. The choice is yours! Be advised that I hereby wash my hands from this man's blood!"

Without another word spoken by Pontius, Antipas, or any of the seventy assembled, the priests quietly filed out.

Part 12
The Crucifixion

Jesus' Address

When great vengeance was sought for a victim, the choice of death was usually the crucifix. And this was the choice of execution chosen by the Sanhedrim for Jesus. In this manner, they would not only have their satisfaction, but they would be able to reestablish fear into the hearts of the followers of Jesus, showing what happens when they made Jehovah angry.

The place of execution usually selected was a nearby hill called Golgotha, which meant "Place of the Skulls."

It was about noon of the next day when thousands of people gathered to see the tragic event. Some came to condemn him. Some came to show their love for him. But most came out of curiosity. Word had spread throughout the land that the "miracle messiah" had been condemned to death, and these thousands wanted to be an eyewitness to what miracle he would perform to free himself.

Thousands more gathered outside of the city's gate, fearing to enter into Jerusalem.

After all, they had heard this was the son of Jehovah and they feared what wrath Jehovah would bring down on the city for killing his only begotten son.

The Roman guards were numerous, enclosing the place where the procession was forming. Both sides of the street were densely packed with people. People also hung from every doorway, window, porch, and rooftop.

As Jesus appeared, he saw many of the women who had attended his sermons and could see how they were bitterly weeping. He asked one of his escort guards to go to Pontius and to ask if he could address this small group for one last time. The guard did as requested.

A few minutes later, Pontius appeared and announced Jesus would be permitted to speak his farewell. Caiaphas stepped forward and protested viciously, however, the governor would not be overruled this time.

Jesus was led up several of the marble steps so all could see him, and with a loving look, he addressed these gentle women.

"Weep not, mothers and daughters of Jerusalem; weep not for me! Rather weep for yourselves, your sons, your husbands, brothers, and fathers. For me there is no occasion to weep. All is peace and tranquillity within me. I have long seen the errors and unhappiness of our people and I have attempted to show the cause of this.

"My words and my love to you all shall not die! Although I as a mortal man shall be no more, through you, my love and my teachings will continue!

"My enemies think that when they have sacrificed my life, they will destroy the influence and knowledge I have shared with you, but be well advised that I realize it will be through your love, my knowledge lives and will grow!

"Yes, women of Jerusalem, after I have drunk from the cup of death, my spirit goes to another world far superior to this. Where I go, my enemies cannot come until they reform thoroughly.

"Those who forsake the darkness of Mosaical superstition and aspire to the true wisdom of your Godlike attributes, a world of beauty will open to you, and there we will embrace one another once again in friendship and love!

"Now, my dear sisters, it is time to say God be with you! My only regret is the time will come when the two tribes of Israel will be scattered to the four winds. Their name as a nation shall be lost and will be found to be scorned by many nations. All that is noble will be lost and the only man who endeavored to save them was put to death! Woe, woe to Jerusalem!"

Jesus, having ended his address, was led back down the steps and to the spot where he was to begin dragging his cross.

A New Hope

As Jesus started out, he was met with an unusual quietness, but as the minutes passed, some of the observers began to call out, "Perform a miracle!" "Call on you father, Jehovah!" "Son of Jehovah, kill your enemies!" Soon the noise reached a crescendo with the thousands eagerly anticipating what great thing was about to occur.

As Jesus struggled past, Mary made a desperate push to break out from the crowd and be at his side, but the attempt was quickly aborted, with her being restrained by the guards who lined the street.

Judas, who was present in the crowd with Cosbi, saw her anguish and also noted she had no one to offer her any degree of comfort. He motioned for Cosbi to join him as he made his way toward her.

Even though she was surrounded by a tremendous crowd, she had never felt so alone and so empty in her life. Over and over again, she moved down the line and kept calling out to Jesus to let him know she was there with him, but it was to no avail. In his great pain and with all of the senseless screaming, he was not able to detect the gentle voice of Mary, even though she exerted her voice with every fiber of her body. Neither was he even able to get a glance of her as sweat filled his eyes. All that he was now aware of was the same hopeless pain Mary was experiencing.

Turning, she saw Judas, the one person she had always believed was her true friend. Being so hopelessly alone, she buried her face into his shoulder and wept. As she put her dainty arms around his neck, Cosbi's eye's grew wide when he saw her bracelet. He instantly remembered he had seen another one just like it many years previously.

As she raised her face back to the street, she saw Jesus had moved further down. She pulled away from Judas to continue her pursuit to let Jesus know she was there with him.

Cosbi took this opportunity to pull Judas aside. Knowing he would not be able to hear, he motioned for them to move away down a side street where they could speak.

Moving to a point where the din was not so great, he asked Judas, "That bracelet!

Where did she get it?"

Judas gave Cosbi a strange look, wondering why he was making such an ordeal about nothing. In following him, he believed perhaps Cosbi had come up with some great trick which might save Jesus even now.

"Why do you ask such a foolish thing?" Judas demanded.

"Believe me," he responded, "if there is anything that might save him at this point, it would be that bracelet!"

As Judas listened, Cosbi explained how he had been in the service of a great female healer many years previously. He explained she was an exceptional woman of a very noble background and although she seldom spoke of her earlier years, he knew she had a connection to royalty because of the bracelet she wore.

She had once told him there was only one other exactly like it in the world. She had asked that if in his journeys he should ever see it, he should question that person and ask them to return with him to her home.

She also informed him she would make it well worth their effort, offering them great wealth for any information they had about the bracelet. She explained this belonged to her son of whom she had lost track while in his infancy.

Judas's eyes widened. "Glaphira!"

"You know her?" Cosbi asked in astonishment.

"I know of her! Before his mother died, she told him of his royal heritage. It was this reason his followers seemed to be so dedicated to him. They believed he would one day reclaim his heritage, and they figured that since they were so dedicated, they would gain great estates and titles.

"Of course, what upset them the most was the fact he kept this to himself. It was not until long after the others had began to tell stories of him becoming the 'king of the Jews' that he finally admitted it, but still, he never made an attempt to contact either parent."

"But perhaps she can assist us now!" Cosbi beamed.

Hope grew in the heart of Judas. "Is she in Jerusalem?"

"She is not far! She stays well hidden even in these days, but she is close by."

"Quickly, dear Cosbi," Judas said as he motioned in the direction that was not crowded, "lead me to her! If any can save him now, it will be her!"

The Return of Glaphira

In a small village not far from Jerusalem, Cosbi led Judas to a humble abode.

When the woman came to the door, her face lit up.

"Cosbi, my dear Cosbi! My faithful assistant! It brings joy to my heart to see you again after so many years!"

"My dear Glaphira," Cosbi said as he embraced her, "I have some news to make your heart even more joyful! I have found your son!"

Her hands shook as she raised them to her shocked face. "My son! I had given up hope! I thought surely I would never see or hear of him again!"

"But there is a bad side, my dear friend," he added. "You have heard of the prophet, Jesus?" She nodded her head slowly. "My dear Glaphira, he is your son! But he has recently been brought to trial and even as we speak, I fear his fate of death is being sealed! At this moment, he is being crucified!"

Horror filled her face. "I have waited all of these years to be with my son! Now that he has been found, do the fates say I am to give him up so easily? No! We must do something!"

"Wise Glaphira, I knew if any could help us, it would be you! What do you propose we do?"

"There is only one thing left to do," she admitted. "It is the one thing I have desperately avoided these many years! I must approach Antipas!"

Meanwhile, the crucifixion of Jesus had been completed to the utter surprise of the multitude. All were shocked Jehovah had not come to rescue his son.

Glaphira and Antipas Meet Again

As Judas and Cosbi entered the temple quarters of Antipas Herod, led by Glaphira, they were quickly halted by his guards.

After showing the seal of the bracelet, one finally relented and had a servant take her message to Antipas, informing him that a long-time friend had come to see him.

Finally, Antipas entered the alcove and inspected the three of them from a distance.

"And who is it that is supposed to be my long-time friend?" he asked curtly.

"It is I," Glaphira said as she stepped forward. "I am certain I have changed greatly since our last encounter!"

He continued to stare at her.

"I am Glaphira! I was the one you supposedly loved so much! I was the princess of Iturea!"

His face filled with surprise. "I thought you were dead! Neither my father nor I were able to figure how you so completely disappeared!"

"There is much to relate, especially as to the treachery of your father, which you may have known nothing about! But that is not for present discussion. What is important is why I have approached you at this time.

"You knew that I was with child?" He nodded. "Well, to save his life, I attempted to hide him, but I was so successful in hiding him from your father that even I lost contact of him! The couple I entrusted him to were able to keep a secret so well I was never able to locate him or them again!

"I was not able to locate him, that is, until today! I have found our son, but he is in great peril! You must lend your support in rescuing our son!"

"This is all too fast," Antipas remarked as he gave a wave of his hand. "I need to understand what you are saying! First, I am told I have a son. Then I am told he is in danger. What is this about?"

"Antipas," she said as she began to tremble, "our son is the man called Jesus! The man you and Pontius condemned to crucifixion is our son!"

"And how do you supposedly know this!" Antipas demanded.

"He had possession of the documents I prepared for him, as well as one of the bracelets you gave to me! The one that is the twin to this one!" she exclaimed as she held her arm out. "Also, this friend of Cosbi's has admitted to me that he had taken part in stealing these documents, to obey the orders of the man to whom he was in bond. In turn, the documents were turned over to the Sanhedrim!"

"The Sanhedrim?" he asked as a multitude of expressions crossed his face. "You are saying the men of the Sanhedrim had documents which testified to the fact that Jesus was my son? While they stood before me, they already knew who he was?

"I am beginning to understand more clearly why they were so insistent on his conviction! If the truth be known, he possibly could have caused much havoc with their powers and sway over men!"

He was silent for awhile, then he turned pale. "I am not like my father! I do not openly kill those of my own blood!"

Motioning for the three to follow him, he moved quickly across the courtyard and entered the office of Pontius's recording secretary.

"Summon Pontius!" He barked at the startled clerk. "We have made a drastic mistake! Tell him it is of utmost urgency!"

Pontius Gives the Order

A messenger hastened to the private quarters of Pontius Pilate and delivered the message that Antipas was frantic about some event. Fearing it may relate to a disturbance, Pontius quickly sought Antipas and found him in the grand receiving room.

Seeing Pontius, Antipas, who was usually the calmest of men, informed him in a distraught voice what he had just been told.

Pontius also stood amazed to hear they had turned the son of Antipas over to the cunning and deceitful priests.

Both agreed he would be rescued, but there was another matter Pontius had to consider. He desired for them to carry this off without raising the wrath of Caiaphas. Or more importantly, avoiding the report Caiaphas would make back to Rome. It was highly unlikely Tiberius would accept the incredible story that some man condemned to death was all of the sudden discovered to be the prince of the land.

Pontius informed the group he would give the order for him to be removed, but it would be under the cover of night and when most of the crowd had departed.

This gave Glaphira and Cosbi sufficient time to seek the assistance of the Essene brothers, of which Cosbi knew Jesus was a member.

Judas, however, did not join them. He had another very important matter to settle.

Part 13
The Rescue

Judas Confronts Saul

At the base of Mount Olivet, near the tombs carved into the hill, Judas waited for Saul. It was now time for Judas to receive his ultimate payoff. Since the beginning of this escapade he had been indebted to Saul, but now, by Saul's own agreement, he was to be freed from his bond and was to receive a sizable payment.

After waiting for a considerable time, Saul finally made his appearance. "My dear Judas," he said in a gentle voice, "I have come as you have asked. What is it that you desire of me?"

Judas looked a little shocked Saul had so completely forgotten their previous agreement. "I only wish for you to fulfill your promise! You told me that once your goals were reached, you would free me of my bond and reward me sizably!"

Saul continued to smile. "As you have been true to me, I am prepared to fulfill your expectations of me. I have brought you two hundred shekels. That is all I have at present, but I will have more for you tomorrow!"

"And do you have my bond of servitude? That is far more important than this bag of money!"

"I have it," Saul replied. "Happily, I give you your freedom! Here, take it and study it by the light of the moon. Satisfy yourself that all is correct."

Judas took the document and proceeded to examine it. While he was engaged in studying it, he didn't notice Saul had drawn a dagger.

Rolling the scroll back up, he remarked, "You are a man of your word! It has been a long time since I was a free man!"

But just as Judas gave Saul a departing embrace, Saul drove the dagger deep into his side.

"Saul!" Judas cried out, "Your heart is blacker than sin! Why do you do this?!"

Saul pushed Judas to the ground and stood over him, poised, dagger in hand, ready to deal the killing blow.

"Monstrous demon!" Judas moaned. "Why couldn't you have allowed me to depart in peace? After all I have done for you! Have I betrayed your secrets? Have I exposed your evil ways?"

"No, Judas, so far you have not!" Saul said as he glared down on him. "But you know all of my secrets. I still have many more plans in place and I cannot take a chance you might betray me later, not being under bond to me!"

"I curse you Saul," he said as he winced with pain. "Should the doctrines of Jesus be true, as I believe they are, we shall meet again, and when we do--"

Not permitting Judas to finish, he dropped and drove the dagger deep into his chest.

"Poor Judas," Saul said to himself as he stood up. "I regret your death, but I am sure you can understand my reasoning a lot better now!"

He carried the body into the tombs and carefully hid it. Going back outside, he took possession of the scroll and the bag of coins. He then quietly departed.

The True Events of the Resurrection

As the crowd departed, some were very confused, but most were just disappointed. None could understand why some great miracle had not occurred.

In the shades of darkness, a small band of soldiers escorted Glaphira, Cosbi, and three Essene brothers to where Jesus had been crucified.

With help from the guards, they slowly untied his bonds, pulled the spikes from his wrists and feet, then carefully lowered him to the ground.

Brother Nicodemus spread powerful spices and salves on long pieces of cloth. These he wound around the body of Jesus.

From there, they carried Jesus to a sepulcher which had been carved from out of a rocky hillside. This was at a considerable distance, being located near the home of these Essene brothers.

They smoked the grotto with aloe and other strengthening herbs and placed a large stone in front of the entrance so the vapors might better fill the grotto.

Unfortunately, this event had been witnessed by many people and some had followed, desiring to know where the body of Jesus would be placed. The guards were finally able to drive them away, telling them that Jesus was dead and now his friends only desired to spend some time with him alone.

When Caiaphas heard of the early removal, though, he sent two servants to post themselves nearby and report all events to him.

The next morning, one of the Essene brothers, under instruction, returned to check on the condition of Jesus.

He was a brother of the fourth degree and as such, wore a white robe. When the cowardly servants of the high priest saw the white-robed brother on the mountain, undefined in the morning mist, they became frightened, thinking that an angel was descending from the mountain. They ran away and refused to return.

Shortly thereafter, twenty-four more brothers arrived at the grotto and were pleasantly surprised to find that no witnesses were present.

Entering, they found the white-robed novice kneeling down on the moss-strewn floor, supporting the head of the revived Jesus.

Jesus, recognizing his Essene friends, smiled. His eyes sparkled with joy as he attempted to sit up. "Where am I?" he asked.

Nicodemus approached him and informed him of all that had transpired.

After the wrappings were removed and the muckender was taken off of his head, Nicodemus told him, "This is not a place to remain any longer. The enemies might discover our secret and betray us!" But since Jesus was not well enough to walk far, he was led to the house of the Order.

Another novice was left with the first to assist him in annihilating every trace of the wrappings, as well as the drugs and medicines which had been used. They were also told to misdirect anyone who might come looking for Jesus.

The others left, but before the two brothers had completed their task, several women came to the cave and were alarmed that the stone had been removed.

Upon entering, they were further terrified, seeing the two dressed all in white. A couple of them fell to the ground, thinking they had seen angels.

One of the brothers addressed them, telling them Jesus was no longer here. When one of the women asked where he had gone, he said to look for him in Galilee, following his instructions to lead people away from this area.

The Essene friends attempted to persuade Jesus to stay hidden, but Jesus had a great desire to prove to his friends that he still lived. After three days had passed, he was well enough to get up and slowly move around. At this time, he asked for clothing so he could venture outside. He was immediately given an Essene robe.

Mary's anguish only grew at finding that the body of her beloved had been removed from its resting place. It was on her third day of lamenting that Jesus saw her in the distance. His heart leaped for joy, and he hurried as best he could toward her, but it seemed like a never-ending journey. Taking each step, he found that tremendous pain shot through his body.

Finally reaching where she sat, he approached and stood behind her.

When he exclaimed, "Oh, Mary!" she turned, but couldn't believe her eyes. She wanted to kiss his feet and then she tried to embrace him, but the pain was too much for him to bear. Cautiously, he stepped back and informed her of his still serious condition.

Slowly, the two of them walked along the wall until they reached the gate which led into the valley. The women standing there believed that they were seeing an apparition. Word had already spread that the angels had come for Jesus and everyone had heard they told the women he would make an appearance in Galilee.

"Lord!" one of the women shouted out, "shall we obey the word of the angel and see you in Galilee?"

Their question confused Jesus. He wasn't sure what she was saying to him, since he was not aware of the attempt of the brothers to lead people away.

After considering the question for a moment, though, he felt it would be a safe place for him and Mary to go.

"Yes," he said, "inform my friends that if I am able, I will go to Galilee."

Mary was permitted to stay with Jesus at the house of the Essene, and they remained there in secret for a period of two weeks.

At that time, he felt well enough to make the journey. Although the brothers asked him to wait awhile longer, he was insistent and they finally agreed to assist him.

Two brothers volunteered to travel with them, but Jesus declined the offer. After much insistence on the part of the Essene, he finally agreed to make contact with members as the two of them traveled along.

Caiaphas heard constant rumors that Jesus had been seen in many different places. This was upsetting for more reasons than one.

Many of the people of the city believed Jesus had risen from the dead by the hand of God, and they began to complain about the injustice that had been done. Caiapas feared the people might revolt, so he was strictly on his watch.

To protect his position, he planned to send assassins once he knew the exact location of Jesus.

When Jesus declared his intention to step forth in Galilee, in places where he had been known before, the Essene friends persuaded him to not do so, explaining the great danger he would face.

The people, however, desired very much to see Jesus, so he made arrangements by letting some of his followers know where he would go to bid the people farewell. This was in a place considered safe, being a lonely stretch of land where he had not previously appeared.

When hundreds of people appeared, the Essene brothers became very nervous, stating an assassin could be in their midst, but Jesus assured them this would be his last public address.

Jesus descended from the summit of the mountain, where the fog assumed a reddish color from the sun, and since he wore the white robe of the Essene order, the people imagined him to be a supernatural being and bowed down, with their faces to the ground.

As Jesus spoke in a loud and clear voice, he asked them to rise and to know there was no difference between them and himself.

"Know that we all are from the same God, the God of love and mercy! Know that there are many kingdoms beyond this one, and know that with Spirit, you will never walk alone!

"Be of good cheer and firm in your faith! Know that my mission in this world was not to form any radical superstitions, but only to teach the truths as they have been shown to me.

"I leave you now and will never see you again in this world. But know that we shall be together again in a much better world. It is not a world of just my Father, but the Father of us all!"

A messenger arrived seeking out an Essene elder while Jesus spoke. He informed the elder the secret messengers of the priests and the grand council had been told of the excitement and some were on their way at this very moment.

Finally, as Jesus completed his address, two of the brothers approached him and escorted him back up the misty mountain to safety. The public would never see him again.

Through the assistance of the Essene, Mary and Jesus would seem to just disappear off the face of the earth. Under the protection of the brothers, even those who realized Jesus had survived the cross would be convinced he died a short time later.

Those who were present at his last public meeting knew the truth, that Jesus was protected by his Essene brothers, but others chose to insist Jesus had arisen from the dead and would say he rose on a cloud, escorted by two angels.

Part 14
Saul, the Showman

Saul's Conversion

As Saul decided it was time for him to go public, he realized he would be a man walking a tightrope. He knew it would be extremely difficult to enter among the disciples, gain their trust, take hold of the mantle of leadership to which he felt he was entitled to, and still not fall victim to the priests.

First of all, he endeavored to convince the Sanhedrim his dedication was to them. This he did by making murderous threats against the disciples. He even took a major part in having several minor individuals put to death by a random stoning, saying they had committed blasphemous remarks about Jehovah. Even though illegal, stonings were still prevalent.

Cosbi still worked closely with Saul, even after Judas had so mysteriously disappeared, but Saul realized his circle of trust would need to be greatly expanded. Through Cosbi's careful assistance, an intriguing cast of actors was assembled.

Caiaphas, coming to trust Saul completely, permitted him to continue laying out the plans designed to discourage the followers. Saul informed him it would be far easier for them to trap rodents with cheese than with poison.

The high priest listened intently as Saul carefully plotted his next endeavor.

His plan was to display some form of 'change of heart'. All of the sudden, he would have a complete turn around and become a follower of this Jesus, who had supposedly risen from the dead. This would give him an edge in attempting to destroy the new following from the inside.

Saul was quite pleased when Caiaphas admitted it would take something almost as great as a resurrection to gain their trust now. For he knew Saul was well known as a prosecutor of the faith.

"You are very correct," Saul confided. "It is for this reason we must take extreme care to not allow any of the Sanhedrim to take action against me, for saying the things I must and even for performing some so-called miracles in the name of the now dead Jesus.

"I will pretend to be carrying out a service for you, when all of the sudden I will become engaged in some wonderful miracle. This, in turn, will bring enlightenment to me with a wonderful conversion to the faith.

"All I will need on your part is a squad of four of your soldiers and a few of your paid men."

Caiaphas admitted that was a low enough price to pay, but wanted more of an in-depth explanation.

"The plan I have devised will call for your demanding the arrest of some of the followers who reside in Damascus. It will become known that I and the squad have been sent by you to arrest men and women alike. But that is only the first stage. With the help of my assistants, some miracle will be staged that completely converts me.

"It will be at this point I will need the assistance of your paid men. I doubt any would believe my act if I didn't raise the wrath of the priests in some way."

The plan met Caiaphas's enthusiastic approval.

Arriving in Damascus, a great crowd turned out to watch the event which had been previously announced by Saul's assistants, the arrest of the Christian men and women.

Coming to the center of the village, Saul suddenly let out a dreadful scream and threw himself from his mount.

He began to roll about and thrashed violently while continuing to scream. "The light! That blinding light! And the noise! Do you hear that thunderous sound!"

Even his squad of soldiers were speechless at the sight of this most extraordinary event. The people all looked at one another. No one saw or heard anything except for the show Saul was putting on.

At length, he cried out that he was blind. One of the soldiers rushed to help him get to his feet. He proclaimed that the Son of God had approached him in a flash of light and had asked why the followers of Jesus were being persecuted. And now, due to the bright flash of divine light, he had been left blind.

The people fell in behind the horses and began to follow them as the soldier led the supposedly blind Saul to a prearranged location.

One of Cosbi's close associates, called Ananias, had been planted there many weeks previously and had already begun to make a name for himself by proclaiming the miracles of the risen Christ.

Coming into the crowd who had gathered outside of the house where Saul had been led, Ananias announced in a loud voice that the voice of the Lord had overcome him and instructed him to go to this man Saul. He even claimed the Lord had told him where to find Saul.

"When the Lord came to me," Ananias said, "and told me to go to this man to help him regain his sight, I told the Lord about the many accounts I have heard where this Saul had done much harm. But the Lord told me, 'Go! This man is my chosen instrument to carry out my name before the Gentiles and their kings and before the people of Israel. I will show him how much he must suffer for my name!'

"So it is that I come before you to assist Saul in regaining his sight!"

Followed by a crowd, Ananias entered the house, approached Saul, and laid his hands over his blind eyes.

Ananias announced, "Saul, Jesus who appeared to you as you entered into Damascus has sent me here so that you may see again!"

To everyone's shock, Saul instantly announced he could see.

Saul spent several days among the followers who lived in Damascus and asked for permission to speak in the synagogues. He now proclaimed that Jesus was the Son of Jehovah and he had returned so he could continue to perform miracles through his disciples and chosen Apostles.

All who heard him were astonished and asked, "Isn't he the man who raised havoc in

Jerusalem on the followers and then came here to arrest many of our men and women?"

The people, believing him to be a devout Jew, were baffled by all of these sudden changes.

On Saul's instruction, his company of men began to speak out against him, stating that they planned to put him to death. They then posted themselves at the city gate to make sure he would not escape.

In this demonstration, none seemed to question why they waited at the gate instead of going directly to him.

However, the story seemed to be far more dramatic for him to escape by being lowered in a basket from the city wall.

Saul Encounters the Disciples

When Saul arrived back in Jerusalem, he immediately attempted to join the disciples, but they were afraid of him.

His friend, Barnabus, took him to them and related the story about the events which had occurred in Damascus, complete with his encounter of the vision of Jesus, his conversion, and how he had to escape in fear for his life.

Saul stayed with them and moved about freely in Jerusalem, boldly speaking in the name of Jesus. Caiaphas informed the priests to continue to ignore these speeches.

With no further attacks coming from the Sanhedrim, the teachings of the Way continued to expand throughout Judea, Gailee, and Samaria.

At this point, Saul realized that to win further converts, the miracles would need to continue.

Although Jesus was gone, the stories still persisted that he had risen from the dead. Saul was not sure if Jesus had really survived the cross or if this was the result of mass hysteria, but it didn't matter either way to him. The story was too great a golden opportunity to not take advantage of.

Peter Performs Miracles

When the disciples finally realized Saul might be able to help them gain all of the power and wealth they had been seeking from the start, they eventually recognized him as one of their group.

Peter, with the help from Saul, Cosbi, and Ananias, was the first to be primed for a public demonstration, displaying that he could now perform miracles also.

To Saul's delight, Peter proved to be a great showman also. The four of them traveled to Lydda with the intention of performing a miracle by healing a cripple.

Upon arriving there, Cosbi separated himself from the rest to prepare himself. In the plan, it would be he who would be the paralytic.

At the designated spot, Peter announced to a growing crowd he had come to heal this particular man, having been sent by the risen Lord.

Peter laid his hands on him and said, "Jesus Christ heals you! Get up and walk!"

Slowly, Cosbi began to rise. He wobbled for a few minutes, then began to move about. "Praise be to the Lord God!" Cosbi exclaimed. "I walk! Jesus and Jehovah are one!"

From this action, many more followers were gained in both the cities of Lydda and Sharon.

Later, a woman asked Saul why it was only crippled men and blind men who were healed. She asked why Jesus turned his back on the needs of women.

Here Saul saw a flaw he had overlooked. He decided the next miracle would be a woman, but it would need to be an extra special display.

The sister of Ananias proved to be the equal to any man in the company when it came to staging a good show.

Tabitha lived in Joppa, near Lydda, so Peter announced to the masses that the Lord had once again descended upon him and told him to go to Joppa, where he was instructed to raise a dead woman.

Since this had worked so well before, by pure accident, Saul felt it was time for another resurrection.

Hundreds now followed him as he set out to perform the miracle of miracles.

When they arrived at the chosen place, Peter was informed the body of the dead woman would be found in an upstairs room. It was a room which overlooked the street and displayed many windows.

The three went upstairs while many attempted to follow. The door and the stairs were blocked by the dozens who desired to get a better view.

Putting his hands on Tabitha, he commanded, "By the power of the risen Christ, I command you to rise!"

A tremendous gasp spread when she opened her eyes and sat up.

Peter took her by the hand and helped her up. He then led her to the windows to show the crowd outside she was alive again.

The news of this marvelous event quickly spread throughout the land, and shortly the dedicated followers numbered in the thousands.

Saul Becomes Paul

While in Cyprus, Saul chose to change his name to Paul. This he did to recruit and influence Sergius Paulus, the proconsul of Cyprus. In addition, he realized it was time to separate himself from his previous identity as a persecutor of the followers.

As Saul spoke to Paulus, Cosbi appeared dressed in a long, dark robe and carrying a staff. He announced, "I, Elymas, the sorcerer, proclaim that you, Saul, have no powers to match mine! Your powers are weak! I advise the proconsul to turn his head from you! Be gone or my powers will destroy you!"

Saul, who now chose to be called Paul, looked straight at the sorcerer and informed him, "You are a child of the devil and an enemy to everything that is right! You are filled with all kinds of deceit and trickery! Now the Lord, through me, stands against you! You shall now be blind and for a time, you will be unable to see the light of day!"

With a quick wave of Saul's hand, Cosbi began to grope about, proclaiming he could not see and begged to be forgiven.

The proconsul watched in shocked and horrified amazement. He was converted on the spot and remained dedicated to Paul for the rest of his life, offering his service in the recruitment of further converts.

Part 15
Further Expansion

A New Embellishment

Paul began to expand his sermons to now include the Gentiles as well as the idea that Jesus had died for their sins. "The great God Jehovah gave his only son in a blood sacrifice so that you may be freed from the sins that you have committed," Paul proudly announced.

The Gentiles, hearing this, became highly honored that this man Jesus was so willing to pay so great a debt for them. The Gentiles flocked to become followers.

In Lystra, as Paul was speaking, he brought attention to a man sitting on the ground. He asked the man, who again was Cosbi, if he had the ability to stand. Cosbi informed the group he could not, that he had been lame even from birth.

Paul looked directly at him and called out, "Stand up on your feet!" With that, Cosbi jumped up and began to walk.

When the crowd saw what Paul had done, they shouted out, "The gods have come down to us in human form!"

Barnabus they called Zeus, and Paul they called Hermes because he was the chief speaker.

The crowd circled them, offering sacrifices and begged to be accepted as followers.

Upon returning to Jerusalem, Barnabus and Paul told the others about the great potential which faced them by expanding the teaching, stating that Jehovah was the God of all mankind and not just the Jews.

Baranabus informed them of Paul's new embellishment that Jesus had died for all mankind. He said this would open the door to a greater following, which would further improve their growing status. This pleased them greatly. Paul was giving them what Jesus had failed to give.

Jesus Becomes the "Unknown God"

While in Athens, Paul noted how very religious and open-minded the people were. In the Parthenon, he saw many shrines dedicated to various gods. He also noted that in addition to the many gods, there was one shrine dedicated to the "Unknown God." They did this to make sure no god would be overlooked.

A most marvelous idea came to Paul. Through this shrine, he could proclaim that Jesus was that Unknown God. Jesus had now gone from merely being the Son of God, to being God Himself.

He attended a meeting of the Areopagus, which was comprised of teachers who possessed a profound knowledge of spiritual matters.

When questioned about this strange new teaching, he stood up in the meeting and said, "Men of Athens! I see that in every way you are very religious. For as I walked around and observed your objects of worship, I even found an altar with the inscription: To An Unknown God. Now what you have been worshipping as something unknown, I will introduce to you.

"The God who made the world and everything in it is the Lord of heaven. Seeing the sins and problems of men, he entered into this world through the body of an infant who had been born from the womb of a virgin!

"He walked among all men, performing endless miracles everywhere he went. He made the blind see, the crippled walk, and on occasion raised the dead to show the power of his divine being! Even when the priests of Israel killed him, he rose from his tomb and continued to walk among men, teaching them of his divine powers, forgiving them of their sins!"

When they heard about the resurrection of the dead, some of them sneered, but others said they wanted to hear more on this subject again at a later date.

At that, Paul left the council. A few men of the council became followers of Paul. Among them was Dionysius and a woman named Damaris, plus a few others.

In Corinth

Paul found that Corinth was a breeding ground for people of low morals and that he could easily convert the people with the promise of "forgiving them for their sins." Coming from the very pious Jews, he was very surprised to discover that at the Temple of Aphrodite, prostitution was actually their form of worship.

Here, he had more freedom to try out his "new acts." He now added a flair to his performances.

With various actors, he began to display healings which were centered on the concept of demons causing illness. When his people, who would be dressed in various disguises, would approach him to be cured from some most horrible infliction, he now used a cloth which he placed over the person's head. He placed his hand on top of the cloth and demanded in the name of God that the demon be drawn up and trapped inside the cloth. The cloth would then be set on fire to the cheers of the onlookers.

He spent two years there but was forced to depart when he collided with the wealthy temple which had continued to be the major religion. Being very jealous of their tremendous wealth, he became a thorn in their side, forever making false accusations toward them. Finally, he informed the temple that if they would offer tributes to his teaching, he would stop the attacks.

Instead, the temple brought charges against him, insisting he was "persuading the people to worship in ways that were contrary to the law."

In Ephesus

Paul claimed he and God were always in direct communication and it was due to this that he possessed divine powers. Handkerchiefs and aprons which had touched him were taken to the sick with the promise that the evil spirits would eventually be driven from them.

Here Ananias went around claiming to drive out evil spirits by using such aprons and invoking the name of Jesus. He also told absurd tales about how he had engaged the evil one.

"When I once removed the evil one, himself," Ananias informed the hundreds who had gathered to hear him, "he told me he knew Jesus and he knew Paul, but he did not know who I was. I informed him I was Ananias, a prophet of the Lord Jesus. To this, the evil one laughed and called on other evil spirits to assist him.

"Calling on our Lord, the victim sprang from his bed and stood beside me. Then with the fury of the Lord within him, he leaped on the evil beings and gave them such a beating they ran out of the house, naked and bleeding!"

As incredible as the story was, many of the Jews and Greeks who lived in Ephesus were seized with fear and the name of the Lord God, Jesus, was held in high honor.

Eutychus Raised from the Dead

In most places people had only heard of the miracles supposedly occurring and demanded to see them for themselves. The endless stories, while they had been interesting, now seemed to just anger many.

Such was the case in Troas. To avoid any difficulty and to assist Timothy with the group he had formed, Paul traveled there under the pretense he had been called to bring a young man back to life.

The story the people had been told was that Eutychus, who in secret was another of Saul's growing company, had been sitting in the window of his third story house when he fell asleep, slipped, and fell to his death.

Arriving at the house, Paul requested the body of the young man be brought down from his room and placed on the same spot where he had fallen. While suggesting this was done for some magical reason, the real reason was so the people of the village could better view the miracle.

When the man was properly placed, Paul lowered himself over the supposed corpse, laying completely on him. This was another new twist added for a theatrical effect.

He put his arms around the youth and held on tightly for a short period of time.

When he stood up, he announced to the people, "Do not be afraid! This man lives again!" That was the clue for Eutychus to begin moving and then to slowly stand up.

The entire audience gasped at the sight of a dead man rising and many ran away, terrified.

On the other hand, Timothy noticed Saul seemed to be bored with these performances. Saul walked inside, broke bread, and ate, while the excitement continued outside.

More and more, his troop began to notice something was becoming seriously wrong with Paul. Some suggested perhaps his guilty conscious was beginning to catch up with him. Others thought he might be bored. It was very difficult to stage a miracle that would be greater than a resurrection.

Part 16
Paul's Final End

The Return to Jerusalem

As time wore on, Paul seemed to slowly lose his reasoning. He traveled extensively, endlessly assisted the disciples in their various districts, and he found himself forever under attack by various forces. Through this and other stress, he became highly suicidal.

Against the advice of his comrades, he even returned to Jerusalem, where he knew he would undoubtedly be confronted with the wrath of Caiaphas for his obvious betrayal of the Sanhedrim. Even though he faced the possibility of death, he seemed to hope for it.

This act left his company in confusion. Some reasoned he might be repenting for all he had done, but most viewed his actions as being due to exhaustion.

After arriving in Jerusalem and being warmly welcomed by the elders of the church, he went to the temple to address the people.

Within minutes, a collection of men dedicated to the priests brought an attack against him. They stirred up the whole crowd and seized him, shouting, "Men of Israel, help us! This is the man who turns all people everywhere against us! His presence defiles this holy place!"

They dragged him from the temple and immediately the city gates were shut.

While they were trying to kill him, news reached the commander of the troops that the whole city of Jerusalem was in an uproar. He took officers and soldiers and ran down into the crowd. When the rioters saw them, they stopped beating Paul. The commander reached Paul and placed him under arrest.

The next day, he was led before the Sanhedrim, but the attacks were so vicious the Romans had to quickly remove him again.

Many of the Jews formed a conspiracy and bound themselves with an oath to not eat or drink until they had killed Paul. More than forty were involved in this plot.

When the Roman commander heard of this, he took Paul to stand trial before the governor, who was now Felix. He listened to what Paul had to offer, but already had his mind made up that he would be found guilty.

When Paul completed his plea about all of the good he had brought to the land, Felix, with a boring brush of the hand, said he would call for him when he wanted to speak to him. Then, as a favor to the Sanhedrim, he left him in prison for two years.

Paul is Returned to Rome

When Felix was replaced by Festus as governor, Festus then sent Paul as well as some other prisoners to Rome.

After many other trying ordeals, Paul finally arrived. Conditions were greatly improved for him in his new prison. After a period of three days had passed, he was even allowed to continue to address those who cared to listen.

When Nero heard of the many things Paul claimed, even including raising the dead, the emperor desired to speak with this interesting person.

Although Nero failed to believe all of Paul's claims, he did find him highly entertaining and gave permission for him to reside in the palace.

Later historical accounts would say Paul angered Nero with his teachings, but nothing could be further from the truth. Nero didn't find Paul's teachings the least bit threatening to the Roman empire. In fact, he found these stories most amusing and even asked Paul to tell some of his outrageous accounts to his guests when entertaining.

To the disciples and to his many assistants, it seemed Paul just decided to give up. It was as if he deliberately made attempts to have himself killed. Over and over again he would insult Nero in his stories, but this only led Nero and his guests to roar with laughter.

Finally, in front of Nero, he made advances to one of his concubines. This is what led him to have his head chopped off.

But in the true style that Paul had set in glorifying events, the stories of his magical abilities were related even in the account of his death.

It was said that when his head was chopped off, he bled milk instead of blood. The story also said his head bounced three times when it hit the ground, and a spring of water sprouted up at each spot the head touched.

The Disciples' Bitter End

Of the original thirteen disciples, only two lived to an old age. They were John and Mary.

Besides Judas, each of the other ten also met horrible and gruesome endings. This, again, was attributed mostly to the absurd stories they insisted on telling, failing to offer the public a sufficient amount of visual evidence.

Instead, the people were forced to listen to outlandish stories, such as the one told about the time Paul met a talking lion in the wilderness, or the one where Andrew claimed to have destroyed an entire race, drowning them in blood.

In Paul's lion account, he claimed that when he was confronted by a lion, he discovered the lion could talk, and it asked to be baptized! Paul supposedly complied, baptizing him on the spot. Then later, when he was thrown into an arena for sport, he found out it was with the lion he had baptized. The lion, recognizing him, bowed before him, astonishing the emperor.

In Andrew's account, he claimed to have been to a mysterious land called Mermadon, where the populace worshipped only the evil one. He went there to save Thomas, who had been captured by these cannibals.

When they captured him also, they dragged him before their idol. He said he would punish them for turning against the Lord Jehovah and with a wave of his staff, blood began pouring from the mouth of the gigantic idol which towered over the city. This, he claimed, killed most of the people by drowning. Those few who survived became dedicated followers.

And with stories such as these, these men were finally put to the test. The disciples seemed to lack Paul's extraordinary gift of showmanship, though. With so many miracles being performed, the people wanted to see for themselves. Each was finally tested by having his own life put on the line by the demanding people. The people figured that if these miracle workers could save the world, they certainly could save themselves.

None passed the test.

Part 17
The Essene Account

Jesus and Mary Finally Together

Once Jesus made his reappearance, the Essene realized that Caiaphas and the Sanhedrim would not rest until Jesus was finally assassinated, so they openly said Jesus had died less than six months after his last sermon. While the Essene were noted for never lying, there was some degree of truth in what they were saying. Without clarifying what they meant by death, they said he was no longer among them. With Jesus deciding that his ministry was over, he had died being the teacher, and with him leaving his homeland to never return again, he considered himself dead to their memory.

It was for this reason that even those who believed he lived after the crucifixion were led to believe he died shortly thereafter, due to his wounds.

With the tremendous love he had for Mary, he was finally able to ask her to be his wife. They were wed by an Essene elder and then sought refuge in distant lands.

When Jesus was between sixteen and twenty, he had become fascinated with the merchant caravans. It was during this four-year period that he traveled with them to the Far East, visiting such places as India and Tibet. And it was due to these wonderful memories from his youth that he decided this would be the destination for his wife and himself.

They spent some time traveling about and traveled extensively in Tibet. Later accounts would verify this through Buddhist scrolls. Modern day explorers have even found drawings of Jesus and Mary in the Nubra Valley of Tibet.

The true Essene account concludes with them finally settling in the land of Cashmere. In his final years, Jesus became a close consul to the king of that land.

They had five children, three sons and two daughters, and lived in peace for the balance of their lives. As a further precaution though, he adopted the name of Isa.

Both of them lived to an old age and when they did reach the end of their lives, they were buried in a specially prepared tomb where they could be placed side by side for all of eternity.

Jesus' final inscription did not read King of the Jews, but said instead, Isa, The Wonderful Prophet.

From Jesus' Essene Brother

"As the brothers rescued Jesus, very little time was wasted. It had been learned by an elder brother that Caiaphas had sent three assassins to get rid of Jesus by whatever means possible.

"A temple assistant who was Essene friendly had heard Caiaphas give the order to them to not return if they should fail in their attempt. If Jesus lived, they would die--and Caiaphas assured them that this time it would not take a Roman order to see to their destruction.

"Instructions were so bold as to say that if they were unable to approach him in private, they should attempt to kill him in public. Caiaphas then assured them he would see to it the Zealots were blamed. Jesus had also angered them by saying the Jews were not fit to be free men, living in their dark superstitions.

"If not worried about safety for himself, Jesus had to worry about the welfare of his beloved Mary, so he complied fully with the plans of our brothers. Together, with two of our brothers, they departed immediately for the safety of distant lands.

"The assassins hunted for them for several weeks, but our brothers were so clever that we created many false trails for them to follow. The assassins finally decided to return to Caiaphas with the story they had successfully killed Jesus. They reasoned that since he had done such a perfect job of hiding his trail, it was quite apparent he would not risk his life again by making another appearance.

"Our brother, Jesus, who was later known as Isa, desired to share all of the beauty of distant lands with Mary. At the conclusion of their adventure, they settled in Cashmere, where our brother found peace and solitude.

"Isa and his wife lived to a happy old age, having five children. They taught that all people were the children of God and they spoke against religions which attempted to control people.

"While their two daughters spent their entire lives in Cashmere, the three sons traveled throughout Europe. Although they weren't prophets, they became well known in the lands they visited. One became a close associate of a king, advising him on all matters of grave concern. Another married into a royal family, and the third became a teacher and scholar. All of the offspring became married and had families of their own.

"The last time I saw the man we now call Isa and his wife was many years ago. As they escorted me to the small bridge which arched over the brook near their home, I was deeply moved by the tender beauty of their lives. Their children had grown and all moved on, leaving Isa and Mary dedicating their entire lives to one another.

"Brother Isa remarked about how nearly he had lost the balance of this wonderful life and now they just sought to be with one another. One was hardly ever seen without the other close by. Even as I departed, I was moved by how they stood beside each other, holding hands.

"As I departed over the crest of the hill, I took one last look back and saw them wave to me. They were still holding hands. That was my last memory of them. I never saw them again."

Part 18
The Buddhist Account

From the Scrolls

The scholar known to our people as Isa traveled throughout our land with his wife, Mary. He was always welcomed everywhere he went, being of the same nature as our people. He expounded deep and profound thoughts about love and peace which are very much in keeping with the teachings of our Lord Buddha.

He spoke of being born in Jerusalem, the son of a prince and a princess, but was robbed of his birthright through a series of bizarre and unusual events. In later years he taught what he called the perfect philosophy, in that it brought together all of the concepts of creation and finally brought understanding to his people about some of their most complex mysteries.

Although he never bore the title of physician, it was apparent many had turned to him for healing. But having unusual abilities and a tremendous insight into the nature of the cosmos, many people in high positions became afraid of him. Fearing that his wisdom could topple their empire, attempts were made on his life, the most serious occurring when he was sentenced to be crucified on a wooden cross. His life was spared at that point only due to the pure love of a handful of people. Upon leaving our land, he has said he will reside in a land similar to our own.

Jesus in the Himalayas

In 1887 a Russian explorer, while traveling through the Himalayan mountains, was thrown from his horse. His leg was broken and he sought assistance from a nearby monastery. Spending several days there, he enjoyed being read to from the many scrolls they possessed.

In total amazement, he realized the contents from one of these scrolls in particular could rewrite history. It related the complete Jesus story, including how he survived crucifixion and was now known as Isa.

After his revelation, when he arrived back home, several other expeditions from various places set out to see this amazing document. It was reported that dozens of people saw this scroll and were read to from it.

More than a hundred years later, in 1998, Dr. Jeff Salz decided it was time to carry through with this change of history and with a filming crew, traveled to Tibet to prove

Jesus did survive crucifixion.

Mysteriously enough, this particular scroll, plus another which also mentioned Isa, were missing. Within such a great period of time, they had evidently been removed by one of the explorers. One could only imagine the reason. But since no one has ever come forth claiming to possess it, it can only be assumed it was removed so the sanctity of the teachings would be preserved.

Just as in the case of Reverend Alexander Smyth, whose book published in 1899, The Confessions of St. Paul, was squashed by religionists, so too was this item hidden from public examination.

Dr. Salz was not so easily discouraged, though. In his film, Jesus in the Himalayas, it shows him pushing on to find some solid evidence Jesus had been to Tibet after his crucifixion.

This evidence he would finally find at Tibet's highest located monastery in Nubra. Traveling up a distance of eighteen thousand, three hundred and eighty feet, he finally discovered what he had come for.

Inside were drawings of many different deities. Among them was one of Jesus and his wife Mary. Also found within the monastery was a scroll that mentioned the journeys of the man Jesus, who was now known as Isa.

Part 19
Deeper Insight

Statement from Dr. Elsie Morris

"In making copies of rare books and manuscripts in the Library of the Christian Israelites about fifteen years ago. I came across a copy of the wonderful letter that was from an Essene elder in Jerusalem written to his brother elder in Alexandria and copied it as accurately as I could. The treasured wisdom in this and similar libraries of this Order is not available for the public and only accessible to advanced students for their private study and benefit and not to be given broadcast to the world. The theory being held that only the initiated can properly interpret and use occult lore, and men will seek such wisdom as soon as they are capable of making good use of it.

"Despite these teachings, however, I have become so deeply impressed with the importance of this letter and the great interest it will undoubtedly excite among scholars and Bible students the world over, that I have had no hesitation in handing it over for publication."

Dr. Elsie Louise Morris, Los Angeles, February 1, 1919.

Letter Made Public

Written by Dr. B.F. Austin, 1920: "After carefully perusing the manuscript for some time, I conclude its contents would interest most deeply too large a section of humanity to allow the Essene letter to remain in the obscurity of private possession or in the archives of a Secret Order. So I have taken steps to have the introductory articles to be translated into German from Latin by German translators. And into Swedish by the Fellows of the Theosophical Society, who will then Translate it into English.

"This revelation shows that Jesus had so strong a compassion he cast aside the secluded life of the Essene, one which demanded he limit his instructions only to the initiated, and went forth into the world to publicly preach to the multitude. So mighty was the tide of inspiration that surged through his being, so urgent the truth that sought expression through his lips, that he was carried outside the pale of the Monastic Order into a ministry for the whole race.

"Thus we find this eyewitness account to be one of the most important transactions in learning the truth about the life and death of Jesus."

Old Manuscripts Found in Alexandria

Revealed by Dr. J.F. Sasberg, 1880: Through one of the members of the Abyssinian Merchants' Company, an old parchment roll, the deciphering of which had scarcely been begun by a learned man, was found in Alexandria in an old building formerly used by Grecian Monks, in a forgotten and abandoned library. A missionary, in his fanatical orthodox eagerness, tried to destroy the antique document. But it was saved with the exception of a few supplements, and a literal translation of the ancient Latin text was accomplished. This transcript was then sent to Germany under the protection of the Freemasons.

Through the archeological researches in Alexandria, it proved to be owned by the Essene Order.

The learned man who was present when it was found was a Frenchman. He sought to deliver it to the French Academy, however, due to the Catholic officials and the Jesuit Mission in Egypt, this idea was aborted. Once they became aware of the parchment, they attempted to destroy it.

With the assistance of the Pythagorean Society, it was saved from the orthodox dumbhead who searched for it. For some time, it remained in the possession of a German Brotherhood, which we regard as the last remains of the old Essene Wisdom.

Three Translations

Dr. T.S. Muskeegon, Swedish translator: "When a copy of the document came into my possession, I instantly realized its importance. I called this to the attention of the three other members who translated this into English. We realize that all translations necessarily partake some of the personality of the translator, so it has been our aim to make our copy as literal as possible, even sometimes at the expense of proper grammatical construction. Our manuscripts have been carefully compared with the original from which they were made, and we have pronounced them correct.

Trusting that it may prove as interesting and instructive to others as it has been to ourselves, we submit it for those who are seeking facts, leaving it entirely to its own merits, for acceptance or rejection, as it may appeal to one's understanding."

In Conclusion

In reading this book, two questions may be prevalent in the reader's mind. The first would be why so much of the history of Jesus and the disciples has been left out of this account, and the second, undoubtedly, would be in regards to why this knowledge has never been made well known.

To answer the first question, I can only state that I have intentionally leaped over many historical accounts due to the very nature of this book. It was felt that well-documented events did not need to be labored on. This was not intended to be a chronicled presentation, but informative in the aspects which were either slightly known or totally unknown. Also, I did not go into any of the areas which would have been highly speculative. In my sincerest effort, I have attempted to present the story of Jesus in the most accurate manner as humanly possible.

As for the second question, it doesn't take much imagination to realize what the answer might be. There has been endless deliberate and malicious destruction of works which didn't exactly comply with the understanding of the controlling forces. Regardless of how absurd some teachings may be, many works which dared to criticize were doomed. This was explained previously.

That was the very reason Jesus' life was placed in danger! He dared to speak out against Moses, saying he lied to his people, that Moses never parted the Red Sea, and that he created Jehovah based on his own virtues of greed, lust, and anger.

But that is what is still taught today! Who would be brave enough to stand before a congregation of believers even now and say such things?

Jesus denied the existence of Jehovah, but suddenly, he is the son of Jehovah! He made every attempt to show his followers he did not die on the cross, but that only led to the teaching that Jesus not only died on the cross, but he was resurrected, and the church is certainly not interested in seeing any kind of proof which says something to the contrary!

All people have a natural fear of death! There is nothing strange and unusual in this. But the true Christian should understand what Jesus was really against! From the very start, he was abhorred by the idea of the people being controlled through fear! He hated the idea that good people were forced to believe in things which were absurd or foolish because their fear ruled their better part of judgment.

The two strongest pillars of some teachings are the Immaculate Conception and the Vicarious Atonement. What if Jesus taught in this world today and denied these two things? Would he be placing his life in jeopardy? Possibly!

Jesus wanted the people to clear their minds of foolish superstitions so they could become enlightened to the true and beautiful worlds which exist beyond this harsh, physical one!

We know that no star can shoot out a beam and light up a manger. We know that people who have left this world do not have resurrected bodies which get up and walk around. And we know that there is no hell inside of the earth where the toes of bad boys and girls are eaten by fiery demons. We know these and a thousand other things are only lies. It is doubtful that even the teachers truly believe them, but the stories continue, just as the story of Moses has continued! And they will probably continue for some time into the future!

As one last parting thought, I would like to thank my spiritual brother, Antares, and my spiritual guide, Darwin Gross, for the wonderful loving care they have offered to me in the preparation of this book! Through their wonderful assistance to millions, they have shown that beautiful worlds do exist beyond this physical one, and they have shown that miracles are real! God bless!